WILLIAMS-SONOMA

beach house cooking

Good Food for the Great Outdoors

Recipes by
Charles Pierce

Photography by
Chris Shorten

TIME
LIFE
BOOKS

TIME-LIFE BOOKS

Time-Life Books is a division of Time Life Inc.

Time-Life is a trademark of Time Warner Inc. U.S.A.

TIME-LIFE CUSTOM PUBLISHING

Vice President and Publisher: Terry Newell
Vice President of Sales and Marketing: Neil Levin
Director of Acquisitions: Jennifer L. Pearce
Director of Financial Operations: J. Brian Birky

WILLIAMS-SONOMA

Founder and Vice Chairman: Chuck Williams
Book Buyer: Victoria Kalish

WELDON OWEN INC.

President: John Owen
Chief Operating Officer: Larry Partington
Vice President and Publisher: Wendely Harvey
Vice President International Sales: Stuart Laurence
Managing Editor: Hannah Rahill
Consulting Editor: Norman Kolpas
Copy Editor: Sharon Silva
Art Director: Diane Dempsey
Production Director: Stephanie Sherman
Production Manager: Jen Dalton
Editorial Assistant: Cecily Upton
Design Concept: Patty Hill
Food and Prop Stylist: Heidi Gintner
Assistant Food Stylists: Kim Konecny, Judith Wadson

In collaboration with Williams-Sonoma
3250 Van Ness Ave., San Francisco, CA 94109

A WELDON OWEN PRODUCTION

Copyright © 1999 Weldon Owen Inc.
814 Montgomery Street, San Francisco, CA 94133

Library of Congress
Cataloging-in-Publication Data

Pierce, Charles.
    Beach House Cooking : good food for the great outdoors /
recipes
    by Charles Pierce : photographs by Chris Shorten
    p.   cm. -- (Williams-Sonoma Outdoors)
    Includes index.
    ISBN 0-7370-2009-1 (alk.paper)
    1. Cookery. I. Time-Life Books.   II. Title.   III. Series.
TX714.P5395   1999
641.5--dc21   98-29714
                              CIP

First Published in 1999
10 9 8 7 6 5 4 3 2 1

Manufactured by Toppan Printing Co., (H.K.) Ltd.
Printed in China

A NOTE ON WEIGHTS AND MEASURES

All recipes include customary U.S. and metric measurements.
Metric conversions are based on a standard developed for these
books and have been rounded off. Actual weights may vary.

A NOTE ON NUTRITIONAL ANALYSIS

Each recipe is analyzed for significant nutrients per serving. Not
included in the analysis are ingredients that are optional or added
to taste, or are suggested as an alternative or substitution either in
the recipe or in the recipe introduction. In recipes that yield a
range of servings, the analysis is for the middle of that range.

introduction 8

breakfast and brunch | 20

Sunrise specialties from omelets and frittatas, to pancakes and
French toast, to coffee cake and just-baked muffins.

soups, salads, and appetizers | 36

Simply made starters and light but satisfying fare featuring
seasonal produce, fish, and shellfish.

main dishes | 54

From seafood to chicken, robust stews to steaks and kabobs,
cooked both indoors and outdoors.

desserts | 86

Refreshing sweets highlight the bounty of summer, from cooling ices
to fresh fruit tarts, puddings to cookies, cobblers to crisps.

index 107

introduction

"Earth and Ocean seem

To sleep in one another's arms, and dream

Of waves, flowers, clouds, woods, rocks, and all that we

Read in their smiles, and call reality."

—PERCY BYSSHE SHELLEY

the beach environment

At any time of year, the beach extends a rich opportunity to commune with nature. A contemplative stroll along the seam where water meets sand attunes the senses to the most elemental details, from pebbles and shells to shoreline wildlife. Remember to do your part to keep the area pristine by always clearing away any debris following your beachside meals.

Life at the beach is irresistible. The rhythm of the waves; the sweet, salty breeze; the warm sun overhead and sand underfoot: every element coaxes the body into easy relaxation, the mind into serene reverie. Seaside meals also play an important part in this willing seduction. From cooling drinks to sizzling steaks, comforting muffins to lively seafood stews, good food adds another pleasurable dimension to the beach experience.

Respecting Your Surroundings

Cooking and serving any food at the shore demands a sense of responsibility toward the environment. When enjoying meals on the sand, clean up thoroughly afterward, taking special care not to leave behind items that might hurt people or ocean creatures. Acquaint yourself with all local regulations regarding trash disposal, and do your part to help make the shoreline's unique character a lasting legacy.

setting beachside meals

Whether you're serving a lunch on the sand, a dinner on the deck at dusk, or a brunch beside a window that looks out on a storm-tossed sea, nature can add her distinctive signature to your table. Indeed, your own beachcombing will yield all the decorative items you need, including shells, wave-polished pebbles, and driftwood.

Choosing the Right Tableware

The tableware and accessories you choose for beach house meals ideally combine both the decorative and the practical. Select colors and patterns that complement the setting; anything from soft blues and greens to hot tropical hues, from solids to sea-inspired motifs can work. At the same time, keep in mind that casual seaside life can subject serving pieces to rough-and-tumble handling. Nonbreakable dishware and easily washable tablecloths and napkins offer years of reliable, easy-care use.

On grand and small scales alike, nature endows beach-side meals with beauty. Take advantage of your location, setting the table, or a blanket on the sand, to maximize appreciation of the view, the salt air, and the sound of the waves. Compose a center-piece of items gathered on your wanderings, including coastal wildflowers (be sure local laws do not prohibit pick-ing) for an impromptu bouquet. Come nightfall, breezeproof hurricane lamps underscore an air of romance.

beach dining practicalities

Keep comfort and convenience in mind when putting together your meals. Lightweight, sturdy folding beach chairs are ideal for guests who do not want to sit right on the sand. To keep out sand borne by the wind or kicked by revelers, improvise simple weighted covers for serving pieces. Large totes make it easy to carry containers of food and drink from house to beach. And, as anyone who loves spending time at the shore knows, large towels are a must.

Many factors will affect the planning of meals for your beach house, including its distance from home, cooking facilities, and proximity to food markets. At best, the situation will be as easy as cooking at home. At worst, you may have to bring ingredients or prepared food with you. In the latter case, choose recipes you can transport and assemble easily. Pay special attention to keeping perishables safe en route. Pack hot foods in thermoses or in well-sealed insulated containers. Foods requiring refrigeration should be surrounded by packets of artificial ice in an ice chest.

Giving Comfort Its Due

Don't forget comfort. Blankets, tablecloths, or large towels are ideal for providing a barrier between sand and food. Have lightweight folding tables on hand to elevate food above the sand. Beach umbrellas are essential for shade. Broad-brimmed hats will also help keep eyes protected from the sun's glare. For nighttime dining, don't forget breezeproof lighting such as hurricane lamps or tiki torches. Have blankets, throws, or shawls on hand to ward off sudden chills.

beverages

apricot-rum funnies

1 ripe banana, cut into 3 or 4 pieces

1½ cups (12 fl oz/375 ml) apricot juice

1 cup (8 fl oz/250 ml) white rum

¼ cup (2 fl oz/60 ml) lemon juice

1 tablespoon grenadine

ice cubes

lemon slices for garnish

In a blender, combine the banana, apricot juice, rum, lemon juice, and grenadine. Fill the blender with ice cubes and blend until smooth, about 30 seconds. Pour into chilled glasses and garnish with lemon slices.

serves six | per serving: calories 146 (kilojoules 613), protein 0 g, carbohydrates 16 g, total fat 0 g, saturated fat 0 g, cholesterol 0 mg, sodium 5 mg, dietary fiber 1 g

strawberry lime sparkler

4 cups (1 lb/500 g) strawberries, stems removed

½ cup (4 fl oz/125 ml) lime juice

¾ cup (6 oz/185 g) sugar

1 bottle (24 fl oz/750 ml) sparkling mineral water, chilled

1 bunch fresh mint, stems removed

cracked ice

Pick out 8 of the smallest strawberries and set aside. In a blender, purée the remaining strawberries. Pour the mixture into a sieve set over a large bowl and force through the sieve to remove the seeds. Add the lime juice and sugar and stir well. Cover and refrigerate for 1 hour or up to 1 day.

In a large pitcher, stir together the strawberry mixture and the mineral water. Lightly crush the mint leaves. Pack tall glasses with cracked ice and several mint leaves. Fill with the sparkler and garnish with the reserved strawberries.

serves eight | per serving: calories 104 (kilojoules 437), protein 0 g, carbohydrates 27 g, total fat 0 g, saturated fat 0 g, cholesterol 0 mg, sodium 2 mg, dietary fiber 2 g

champagne cocktail

3 passion fruits

1 teaspoon sugar

1 bottle (24 fl oz/750 ml) champagne or other dry sparkling wine, well chilled

Cut off the top of each passion fruit. Using a small spoon, scoop out the pulp into a sieve placed over a small bowl and push it through the sieve. Stir in the sugar. Put 1 tablespoon of the pulp into the bottom of each of 8 chilled champagne flutes. Pour in the sparkling wine and serve at once.

serves eight | per serving: calories 72 (kilojoules 302), protein 0 g, carbohydrates 3 g, total fat 0 g, saturated fat 0 g, cholesterol 0 mg, sodium 7 mg, dietary fiber 0 g

mixed-berry lemonade

8 lemons

1½ cups (12 oz/375 g) sugar

1 cup (4 oz/125 g) mixed berries

8 cups (64 fl oz/2 l) water

cracked ice

Finely grate enough lemon zest to measure 1 tablespoon and place in a large nonaluminum bowl. Squeeze the juice from the lemons and add to the bowl along with the sugar. Stir until the sugar dissolves. Place the berries in the bottom of a large pitcher. Lightly crush with the back of a spoon, leaving some berries whole. Add the lemon mixture and pour in the water. Stir well and pour over cracked ice in tall chilled glasses.

serves eight to ten | per serving: calories 160 (kilojoules 672), protein 0 g, carbohydrates 42 g, total fat 0 g, saturated fat 0 g, cholesterol 0 mg, sodium 1 mg, dietary fiber 1 g

ginger iced tea

For a festive touch, wet the rims of tall glasses and dip in a mixture of finely chopped crystallized ginger and sugar.

1 piece fresh ginger, 3 inches (7.5 cm), peeled and coarsely grated

10 cups (2½ qt/2.5 l) water

1 cup (8 oz/250 g) sugar

¼ cup (1 oz/30 g) loose tea leaves such as English Breakfast or Earl Grey

cracked ice

Place the ginger in a large, nonaluminum bowl. Pour in 4 cups (32 fl oz/1 l) of the water, cover, and let stand undisturbed for 48 hours.

Line a sieve with cheesecloth (muslin) and place over a saucepan. Strain the ginger water through the sieve, then add the sugar to the saucepan. Bring to a boil over high heat, stirring, then reduce the heat to medium and simmer, undisturbed, for 10 minutes. Remove from the heat, stir in the tea, and cover. Let steep for 5 minutes. Strain into a large, heatproof pitcher and pour in the remaining 6 cups (48 fl oz/1.5 l) water. Stir well, cover, and refrigerate until well chilled. Pour over cracked ice in tall glasses.

serves eight | per serving: calories 113 (kilojoules 475), protein 0 g, carbohydrates 29 g, total fat 0 g, saturated fat 0 g, cholesterol 0 mg, sodium 9 mg, dietary fiber 0 g

mango smoothies

2 mangoes, peeled, pitted, and cut into 1-inch (2.5-cm) dice

1 cup (8 oz/250 g) plain yogurt

½ cup (4 fl oz/125 ml) milk

1 banana, coarsely chopped

2 tablespoons lemon juice

1 teaspoon vanilla extract (essence)

Place the mangoes in a plastic bag and freeze until firm, at least 1 hour.

Just before serving, in a blender, combine the frozen mango, yogurt, milk, banana, lemon juice, and vanilla. Blend until very smooth. Pour into chilled glasses and serve immediately.

serves two | per serving: calories 305 (kilojoules 1,281), protein 10 g, carbohydrates 61 g, total fat 5 g, saturated fat 3 g, cholesterol 15 mg, sodium 117 mg, dietary fiber 3 g

breakfast and brunch

blueberry buttermilk pancakes

For best results, have all the ingredients at room temperature and use a light hand when mixing the batter. For a robust breakfast before a late-morning game of beach volleyball, serve the pancakes with butter and maple syrup or honey and accompany with bacon, smoked sausages, or grilled ham steaks.

2 cups (10 oz/315 g) all-purpose (plain) flour

2 teaspoons baking powder

1 teaspoon baking soda (bicarbonate of soda)

1 teaspoon salt

2 eggs

2 cups (16 fl oz/500 ml) buttermilk

¼ cup (2 oz/60 g) unsalted butter, melted and cooled, plus 1–2 tablespoons

2 cups (8 oz/250 g) small, stemmed blueberries

In a large bowl, sift together the flour, baking powder, baking soda, and salt. In another bowl, beat together the eggs and buttermilk until blended. Pour the wet ingredients into the dry ingredients and mix quickly with a large wooden spoon until a smooth batter forms. Fold in the ¼ cup (2 fl oz/60 ml) melted butter and blueberries.

Preheat a large frying pan or griddle to medium-high heat. Brush well with some of the remaining butter and wipe off any excess with a paper towel. Pour or ladle on about 2 tablespoons of the batter for each pancake, forming circles 4–5 inches (10–13 cm) in diameter. Cook until browned on the bottom and bubbles appear on the surface, about 3 minutes. Using a spatula, flip and cook until lightly browned on the second side, about 3 minutes longer. Transfer to a plate and keep warm. Repeat with the remaining batter, brushing the pan or griddle with more butter as needed.

Divide the pancakes evenly among individual plates and serve with desired toppings (see note).

serves six to eight | per pancake: calories 109 (kilojoules 458), protein 3 g, carbohydrates 14 g, total fat 4 g, saturated fat 2 g, cholesterol 32 mg, sodium 276 mg, dietary fiber 1 g

avocado and crab omelets

Omelets should be served as soon as they are cooked. Have all the ingredients assembled, the guests seated, and a stack of warmed plates ready before you begin cooking.

1 large avocado, 8–10 oz (250–315 g), halved, pitted, peeled, and finely diced

1 tablespoon lemon juice

½ lb (250 g) cooked lump crabmeat, picked over for shell fragments and flaked

1 tomato, peeled, seeded, and diced

salt and ground pepper to taste

12 eggs

6 tablespoons (3 oz/90 g) unsalted butter

In a bowl, toss the avocado with the lemon juice. Stir in the crabmeat and tomato. Season with salt and pepper.

In a large bowl, whisk 3 of the eggs with salt and pepper until frothy. In a small omelet pan over medium-high heat, melt 2 tablespoons of the butter. When the butter stops bubbling, add the beaten eggs and immediately stir with the back of a fork until they start to thicken, about 10 seconds. Pull the set portion of the eggs back from the edges and tilt the pan to let the uncooked portion run to the sides. Continue cooking, shaking the pan constantly, until almost set, about 20 seconds longer.

Spoon one-fourth of the avocado mixture onto the center of the omelet. Cook until the bottom is browned and the top is set as desired, 30–45 seconds longer.

Hold the pan handle in one hand and tip the pan away from you. Using a fork, fold the top edge of the omelet over onto the center. Quickly flip the pan over so the omelet slides onto a warmed plate, folded in thirds with the seam side down. Serve at once, then repeat to make 3 more omelets, adding butter to the pan as needed.

serves four | per serving: calories 516 (kilojoules 2,167), protein 32 g, carbohydrates 7 g, total fat 41 g, saturated fat 17 g, cholesterol 741 mg, sodium 357 mg, dietary fiber 1 g

raspberry peach muffins

For variety, substitute strawberries or blueberries for the raspberries, and apricots or nectarines for the peaches.

2 cups (10 oz/315 g) all-purpose (plain) flour

½ cup (4 oz/125 g) plus 2 tablespoons sugar

2 teaspoons baking powder

1 teaspoon baking soda (bicarbonate of soda)

¼ teaspoon salt

1 cup (8 fl oz/250 ml) buttermilk

2 eggs

3 tablespoons unsalted butter, melted and cooled

½ cup (2 oz/60 g) raspberries

1 cup (6 oz/185 g) peeled and diced peaches

🐚 Preheat an oven to 400°F (200°C). Butter 12 standard muffin-tin cups.

🐚 In a large bowl, sift together the flour, ½ cup (4 oz/125 g) sugar, baking powder, baking soda, and salt. In another bowl, whisk together the buttermilk, eggs, and butter until blended.

🐚 Make a well in the center of the dry ingredients. Pour in the buttermilk mixture and then stir quickly to form a smooth batter. Do not overmix. Fold in the raspberries and peaches. Spoon into the prepared cups, filling them three-fourths full. Sprinkle the 2 tablespoons sugar evenly over the tops.

🐚 Bake until a toothpick inserted into the center of a muffin comes out clean, about 20 minutes. Transfer to a rack to cool for 10 minutes, then turn out onto the rack. Serve hot.

makes twelve muffins | per muffin: calories 190 (kilojoules 798), protein 4 g, carbohydrates 32 g, total fat 5 g, saturated fat 3 g, cholesterol 47 mg, sodium 267 mg, dietary fiber 1 g

baked eggs piperade

Piper is the Basque word for "pepper." Add some finely diced air-cured ham, such as prosciutto, to the pepper mixture just before you pour it into the baking dish for an authentic version of this regional favorite.

2 tablespoons olive oil

1 onion, finely chopped

1 celery stalk, peeled and finely chopped

1 large red bell pepper (capsicum), seeded and finely diced

1 large yellow bell pepper (capsicum), seeded and finely diced

1 large green bell pepper (capsicum), seeded and finely diced

1 clove garlic, minced

2 tomatoes, peeled, seeded, and chopped

salt and ground pepper to taste

6 eggs

In a large, heavy saucepan over medium-high heat, warm the oil. Add the onion and celery and sauté until slightly softened, about 3 minutes. Add all the bell peppers and sauté until softened, about 5 minutes. Add the garlic and cook for 1 minute longer. Stir in the tomatoes, increase the heat to high, and bring to a boil. Boil rapidly until the liquid given off by the tomatoes reduces and the mixture is slightly thickened, 5–7 minutes. Season well with salt and pepper, then pour into a 2-qt (2-l) baking dish and spread evenly over the bottom. (The recipe can be prepared up to this point 2 days in advance. Cover and refrigerate until ready to cook the eggs.)

Preheat an oven to 375°F (190°C).

Using the back of a large spoon, make 6 evenly spaced indentations in the pepper mixture. Break the eggs, one at a time, into a small saucer and slip an egg into each indentation, being careful not to break the yolks. Sprinkle with salt and pepper.

Bake until the eggs are soft but not tough and the pepper mixture is bubbling, 20–25 minutes. Serve immediately on warmed plates.

serves six | per serving: calories 160 (kilojoules 672), protein 8 g, carbohydrates 11 g, total fat 10 g, saturated fat 2 g, cholesterol 213 mg, sodium 76 mg, dietary fiber 3 g

french toast with caramelized pears

An old-fashioned cast-iron frying pan works well for caramelizing the pears. Firm cooking apples can be used in place of the pears. Serve the French toast with maple syrup or a light dusting of confectioners' (icing) sugar.

for the pears:

3 large, firm pears, preferably
  Anjou, 1½–2 lb (750 g–1 kg)
  total weight, peeled, cored, and
  finely diced

1 tablespoon lemon juice

½ cup (4 oz/125 g) sugar

1 teaspoon vanilla extract (essence)

2 tablespoons unsalted butter

¼ cup (2 fl oz/60 ml) warm water

for the French toast:

3 tablespoons unsalted butter

2 eggs

2 cups (16 fl oz/500 ml) milk

½ teaspoon vanilla extract (essence)

1 teaspoon sugar

pinch of salt

4 slices brioche or challah, each
  about 1 inch (2.5 cm) thick

To prepare the pears, place them in a bowl and sprinkle with the lemon juice, sugar, and vanilla. Stir to mix, then set aside, stirring often until they begin to give off juices and the sugar dissolves, about 10 minutes.

In a large, heavy frying pan over medium-high heat, melt the butter. Using a slotted spoon, transfer the pears to the pan. Cook, stirring often, until the pears turn a golden caramel color, 20–25 minutes. Pour in the warm water and stir until glossy. Remove from the heat and cover to keep warm. (The pears can be prepared up to a day ahead. Cover and refrigerate, then reheat gently over low heat.)

To make the French toast, in a large frying pan or on a griddle over medium-high heat, melt the butter. In a large, shallow bowl, whisk together the eggs, milk, vanilla, sugar, and salt. Dip the bread slices briefly into the egg mixture, lift carefully to drain, and place in the frying pan. Cook, turning once, until browned on both sides, 6–7 minutes total.

Transfer to plates, top with the caramelized pears, and serve.

serves two | per serving: calories 1,391 (kilojoules 5,842), protein 31 g, carbohydrates 203 g, total fat 53 g, saturated fat 27 g, cholesterol 406 mg, sodium 1,046 mg, dietary fiber 12 g

savory bread pudding with goat cheese and ham

Chopped fresh herbs, if available, can be stirred into the beaten egg mixture just before the pudding goes into the oven.

2 tablespoons unsalted butter,
  at room temperature
24 slices day-old French or Italian
  bread, ¼ inch (6 mm) thick
¼ lb (125 g) fresh goat cheese,
  crumbled
1 thick slice boiled ham, about ¼ lb
  (125 g), finely diced

½ cup (2½ oz/75 g) pitted black
  olives, preferably Niçoise,
  coarsely chopped
6 eggs, lightly beaten
2 cups (16 fl oz/500 ml) milk
½ teaspoon salt
¼ teaspoon ground pepper
boiling water, as needed
2 tablespoons grated Parmesan
  cheese

◯ Preheat an oven to 350°F (180°C). Butter a 2-qt (2-l) baking dish.

◯ Spread a small amount of the butter over one side of each bread slice. Arrange one-third of the bread slices, buttered side up, on the bottom of the prepared baking dish. Scatter half of the goat cheese over the top. Top with half of the ham and half of the olives. Top with half of the remaining bread slices and then layer all of the remaining goat cheese, ham, and olives. Place the remaining bread slices on top.

◯ In a large bowl, whisk together the eggs, milk, salt, and pepper. Ladle or pour the egg mixture over the contents of the baking dish. Cover with aluminum foil. Set the pudding dish in another, larger baking dish and place in the oven. Pour boiling water into the larger baking dish to reach halfway up the sides of the pudding dish.

◯ Bake for 30 minutes. Remove the foil and sprinkle with the Parmesan cheese. Continue to bake until the top is golden brown and the center is set, about 30 minutes longer. Remove from the oven and let cool slightly. Spoon onto individual plates and serve warm.

serves six to eight | per serving: calories 370 (kilojoules 1,554), protein 19 g, carbohydrates 27 g, total fat 20 g, saturated fat 9 g, cholesterol 220 mg, sodium 966 mg, dietary fiber 2 g

scrambled eggs with smoked salmon and chives

Farm-fresh eggs and premium smoked salmon will turn this simple dish into a masterpiece. Serve on a deck overlooking the sea, with toasted bagels and a pitcher of your favorite version of Bloody Marys.

15 eggs

½ cup (4 fl oz/125 ml) half-and-half (half cream)

3 oz (90 g) smoked salmon, cut into narrow strips

4 tablespoons (⅓ oz/10 g) snipped fresh chives

½ teaspoon salt

½ teaspoon ground pepper

◯ In a large heatproof bowl, whisk together the eggs and half-and-half until well blended. Set the bowl over (not touching) barely simmering water in a saucepan. Cook, stirring and scraping the bowl sides constantly with a rubber spatula, until the eggs begin to scramble, 12–15 minutes. Stir in the salmon, 3 tablespoons of the chives, the salt, and the pepper. Continue cooking and stirring until the eggs are soft but not runny.

◯ Quickly transfer the eggs to a warmed shallow bowl, sprinkle with the remaining 1 tablespoon chives, and serve immediately.

serves six | per serving: calories 230 (kilojoules 966), protein 19 g, carbohydrates 3 g, total fat 15 g, saturated fat 5 g, cholesterol 542 mg, sodium 642 mg, dietary fiber 0 g

frittata with caramelized onions and roasted peppers

A frittata, served at room temperature, is perfect for brunch. It can also be wrapped in foil, packed in a cooler, and toted to a beach picnic.

1 large red bell pepper (capsicum)

1 large yellow bell pepper (capsicum)

3 Yukon gold potatoes, about ¾ lb (375 g) total weight

2 tablespoons unsalted butter

2 yellow onions, thinly sliced

¼ teaspoon sugar

pinch of salt, plus ½ teaspoon

6 eggs

¾ teaspoon ground pepper

2 tablespoons grated Parmesan cheese

Preheat a broiler (griller). Cut the bell peppers in half lengthwise and remove the stems, seeds, and ribs. Place the halves, cut sides down, on a baking sheet and broil (grill) until the skins blacken and blister. Remove from the broiler, drape loosely with aluminum foil, let stand for 10 minutes, then peel away the skins and thinly slice; set aside.

Meanwhile, in a saucepan, cook the potatoes in salted water to cover until tender, 30–40 minutes. Drain, peel, let cool, halve lengthwise, and thinly slice.

In a large, heavy frying pan over medium heat, melt the butter. Add the onions, sugar, and the pinch of salt. Cook, stirring often, until the onions are golden brown and lightly caramelized, about 30 minutes.

In a bowl, whisk together the eggs, the ½ teaspoon salt, and the pepper. Arrange the potatoes, overlapping, over the bottom of a large, heavy non-stick frying pan. Scatter over half of the onions and bell peppers. Pour the eggs evenly over the surface, and top with the remaining onions and peppers. Set aside for 20 minutes so that the potatoes absorb some of the eggs.

Place the frying pan over medium-low heat. Cook, shaking the pan often, until the frittata bottom is lightly browned, 10–12 minutes. Slide the frittata onto a large plate, then return it to the pan, browned side up. Cook until lightly browned and set in the center, 2–3 minutes longer. Invert onto a cutting board and sprinkle with the cheese. Let cool to room temperature, then cut into wedges to serve.

serves four to six | per serving: calories 232 (kilojoules 974), protein 11 g, carbohydrates 22 g, total fat 11 g, saturated fat 5 g, cholesterol 269 mg, sodium 614 mg, dietary fiber 3 g

upside-down plum coffee cake

for the topping:

2 tablespoons unsalted butter

½ cup (4 oz/125 g) sugar

½ teaspoon ground cinnamon

4 plums, preferably freestone and
about ½ lb (250 g) total weight,
halved, pitted, and sliced at least
⅛ inch (3 mm) thick

for the cake:

1½ cups (7½ oz/235 g) all-purpose
(plain) flour

1 cup (8 oz/250 g) sugar

2 teaspoons baking powder

¼ teaspoon salt

4 tablespoons (2 oz/60 g) chilled
unsalted butter, cut into pieces

1 egg

½ cup (4 fl oz/125 ml) milk

½ teaspoon vanilla extract (essence)

To make the topping, in a 9- or 10-inch (23- or 25-cm) ovenproof non-stick frying pan over medium-high heat, melt the butter. Stir in the sugar and cinnamon and add the plum slices. Cook gently, stirring, until the plums have exuded their juices and the sugar has dissolved, 5–7 minutes. Remove from the heat and strain through a sieve placed over a small bowl. Arrange the plum slices over the bottom of the frying pan, overlapping them in concentric circles. Reserve the juices.

Preheat an oven to 375°F (190°C).

To make the cake, in a large bowl, stir together the flour, sugar, baking powder, and salt. Using 2 knives or your fingertips, cut in the butter until the mixture resembles coarse meal. In a small bowl, using a fork, beat together the egg, milk, and vanilla until blended. Pour into the flour mixture and stir with a wooden spoon just until a smooth batter forms.

Pour the batter over the plums in the frying pan. Bake until a toothpick inserted into the center comes out clean, about 30 minutes. Invert onto a rack, dislodging any slices that adhere to the frying pan and carefully replacing them on the cake. Brush the top of the warm cake with the reserved juices, then let cool. Cut into wedges to serve.

serves eight | per serving: calories 373 (kilojoules 1,567), protein 4 g, carbohydrates 67 g, total fat 10 g, saturated fat 6 g, cholesterol 52 mg, sodium 211 mg, dietary fiber 1 g

soups, salads, and appetizers

cucumber soup with yogurt cheese and salmon roe

Tiny cubes of peeled and seeded tomato can be used in place of the salmon roe to garnish this low-fat, refreshing soup. Serve as an elegant beginning to a simple meal after a full day at the beach.

for the garnish:

¾ cup (6 oz/185 g) plain yogurt

1 teaspoon grated lemon zest

1 tablespoon snipped fresh chives

salt and ground pepper to taste

for the soup:

2 tablespoons olive oil

1 yellow onion, finely chopped

2 celery stalks, thinly sliced

6 large cucumbers, about 3 lb
   (1.5 kg) total weight, peeled,
   halved, seeded, and cut into
   1-inch (2.5-cm) lengths

2 cups (16 fl oz/500 ml) chicken
   broth

salt and ground pepper to taste

2–3 oz (60–90 g) salmon roe

To make the garnish, rinse a double thickness of cheesecloth (muslin), use to line a small sieve, and place over a small bowl. Spoon the yogurt into the sieve, cover, and refrigerate for 24 hours. The liquid will drain off, leaving behind a smooth, creamy "cheese." Discard the liquid and transfer the cheese to a bowl. Stir in the lemon zest and chives and season with salt and pepper. Cover and refrigerate until serving.

To make the soup, in a large, heavy saucepan over medium-high heat, warm the oil. Add the onion and celery and sauté until tender, about 5 minutes. Add the cucumbers, reduce the heat to low, cover, and cook until tender, about 20 minutes. Pour in the broth and season with salt and pepper. Raise the heat to high and bring to a boil. Remove from the heat, cover, and let cool for 10–15 minutes.

Working in batches, transfer to a blender and blend until very smooth. Transfer to a bowl, cover, and chill well, at least 2 hours. Season with salt and pepper before serving.

Ladle into 4 chilled bowls. Add a dollop of the yogurt cheese and a small spoonful of the salmon roe to each bowl. Serve at once.

serves four | per serving: calories 178 (kilojoules 748), protein 9 g, carbohydrates 15 g, total fat 10 g, saturated fat 1 g, cholesterol 67 mg, sodium 549 mg, dietary fiber 2 g

stuffed cherry tomatoes with crab and tarragon

These stuffed cherry tomatoes are good with drinks before dinner or as part of a cocktail-party menu. Use a combination of red and yellow tomatoes for an attractive presentation.

24 cherry tomatoes, about ¾ lb (375 g) total weight
½ lb (250 g) cooked lump crabmeat, picked over for shell fragments and flaked
1 tablespoon lemon juice

2 teaspoons finely chopped fresh tarragon, plus 24 whole leaves
1–2 tablespoons mayonnaise
several drops of Tabasco or other hot-pepper sauce, or to taste
salt and ground pepper to taste

Cut a slice ¼ inch (6 mm) thick off the top of each tomato and discard the tops. Using a small melon baller, scoop out the seeds of each tomato. Sprinkle the insides with salt and invert onto a baking sheet lined with paper towels. Set aside for 30 minutes to drain.

In a small bowl, mix together the crab, lemon juice, and chopped tarragon. Stir in enough mayonnaise to bind the mixture. Season with hot-pepper sauce, salt, and pepper. Cover and chill thoroughly.

Fill each tomato with a heaping teaspoonful of the crab mixture, mounding the top, and garnish with a tarragon leaf. Serve chilled.

serves four to six | per piece: calories 19 (kilojoules 80), protein 2 g, carbohydrates 1 g, total fat 1 g, saturated fat 0 g, cholesterol 10 mg, sodium 33 mg, dietary fiber 0 g

couscous salad

1 eggplant (aubergine), about 1 lb
   (500 g), trimmed and quartered
   lengthwise

salt for sprinkling and to taste,
   plus ½ teaspoon

4 tablespoons (2 fl oz/60 ml)
   olive oil

ground pepper to taste,
   plus ¼ teaspoon

2 cups (16 fl oz/500 ml) tomato
   juice

1¼ cups (10 oz/315 g) instant
   couscous (1 box)

2 tablespoons red wine vinegar

¼ cup (2 fl oz/60 ml) extra-virgin
   olive oil

25 small cherry tomatoes, about ½ lb
   (250 g), stems removed and halved

2 cups (14 oz/440 g) rinsed and
   drained canned chickpeas
   (garbanzo beans)

2 tablespoons finely chopped fresh
   parsley

8–10 crisp romaine (cos) lettuce
   leaves

Liberally sprinkle the exposed flesh of the eggplant with salt. Set aside to drain on paper towels for 30 minutes. Rinse and pat dry. Brush with 2 tablespoons of the olive oil and season with salt and pepper.

In a large, heavy nonstick frying pan over medium-high heat, cook the eggplant, turning often, until well browned and soft, about 12 minutes. Transfer to paper towels to drain and let cool.

In a large saucepan over high heat, combine the tomato juice, the remaining 2 tablespoons olive oil, the ½ teaspoon salt, and the ¼ teaspoon pepper. Bring to a boil, stir in the couscous, remove from the heat, cover, and set aside for 5 minutes until the liquid is absorbed. Remove the lid, fluff with a fork, and transfer to a large bowl to cool.

Meanwhile, make a simple vinaigrette: Place the vinegar in a small bowl and slowly whisk in the extra-virgin olive oil until an emulsion forms.

Cut the eggplant crosswise into slices about ½ inch (12 mm) thick and add to the couscous. Add the tomatoes, chickpeas, and vinaigrette. Mix well and season with salt and pepper. (The salad can be made to this point up to 2 hours in advance. Cover and keep at room temperature.)

Stir in the parsley. Make a bed of the lettuce leaves on a serving platter. Mound the salad in the center and serve at once.

serves six | per serving: calories 491 (kilojoules 2,062), protein 14 g, carbohydrates 65 g, total fat 21 g, saturated fat 3 g, cholesterol 0 mg, sodium 555 mg, dietary fiber 6 g

curried lobster salad

For a shortcut, buy 1 pound (500 g) cooked lobster meat.
Shaved coconut, which comes in thick curls, is available in most
health-food stores and specialty markets.

3 live lobsters, 1½ lb (750 g) each
2 celery stalks, thinly sliced
⅓ cup (3 oz/90 g) plain yogurt
¼ cup (2 fl oz/60 ml) mayonnaise
1 tablespoon lemon juice
1 teaspoon mild curry powder
pinch of cayenne pepper

salt and ground black pepper
⅓ cup (1½ oz/45 g) shaved
  unsweetened dried coconut
vegetable oil for frying
8 green (spring) onions, including
  tender green tops, cut into 2-inch
  (5-cm) julienne

Bring a large pot three-fourths full of salted water to a boil. Add the lobsters, bring back to a boil, and cook until the shells turn bright red, about 10 minutes. Drain well and let cool.

Working with 1 lobster at a time, twist off the "arms" and break off the claws. Bend the "thumb" of each claw down until it cracks. Using a lobster cracker or mallet, crack the claw shells and extract the meat with a small fork. Crack the "arms" and extract the meat. Using your hands, break the lobster in half at the point where the body meets the tail. Squeeze the sides of the tail together so that the shell underside cracks. With the underside facing you, and one hand on each side of the shell, press open the tail, exposing the meat. Extract it with the fork. Repeat with the remaining lobsters. Cut the meat into ½-inch (12-mm) pieces. Let cool completely. In a bowl, combine the lobster meat, celery, yogurt, mayonnaise, lemon juice, curry powder, cayenne pepper, and salt and black pepper to taste. Mix well.

In a small, dry frying pan over medium-low heat, toast the coconut, stirring often, until golden brown, about 3 minutes. Set aside and let cool.

In a heavy saucepan, pour in oil to a depth of ½ inch (12 mm) and heat until hot (about 350°F/180°C). Add one-third of the green onions and fry until browned around the edges, about 1 minute. Using a slotted spoon, transfer to paper towels to drain. Repeat with the remaining green onions.

To serve, divide the lobster mixture evenly among chilled plates. Sprinkle with the coconut and green onions. Serve immediately.

serves four to six | per serving: calories 294 (kilojoules 1,235), protein 21 g, carbohydrates 7 g,
total fat 21 g, saturated fat 7 g, cholesterol 72 mg, sodium 438 mg, dietary fiber 2 g

tomato tart

This is an adaptation of a recipe made by renowned French chef Georges Blanc. Frozen pizza dough is available in many well-stocked food stores and Italian markets.

1 lb (500 g) pizza dough, thawed if frozen

1 red bell pepper (capsicum)

2 tablespoons olive oil, plus oil for brushing

2 yellow onions, finely chopped

3 cloves garlic, minced

3 or 4 tomatoes, about 1½ lb (750 g), peeled, seeded, and chopped

2 teaspoons chopped fresh thyme

salt and ground pepper to taste

1 cup (5 oz/155 g) pitted black olives, preferably oil cured, halved

Lightly butter a 12-inch (30-cm) springform pan. On a lightly floured surface, roll out or stretch the dough into a 15-inch (38-cm) round. Line the prepared pan with the dough and pinch the edges to form a rim. Set aside in a warm place to rise until puffy, about 1 hour.

Meanwhile, preheat a broiler (griller). Cut the bell pepper in half lengthwise and remove the stem, seeds, and ribs. Place, cut sides down, on a baking sheet and broil (grill) until the skin blackens and blisters. Remove from the broiler, drape loosely with aluminum foil, let stand for 10 minutes, then peel away the skin. Cut into long, narrow strips and set aside.

In a saucepan over medium-high heat, warm the 2 tablespoons oil. Add the onions and sauté until tender, about 5 minutes. Add the garlic and sauté for about 1 minute longer. Stir in the tomatoes, thyme, salt, and pepper. Cook, stirring, until thickened, about 20 minutes. Let cool slightly.

Preheat an oven to 450°F (230°C). Spread the tomato mixture evenly in the dough-lined pan. Arrange the pepper strips over the tomatoes. Lightly brush the edges of the tart with olive oil.

Bake until the edges are golden brown and the dough is cooked through, 30–40 minutes, covering the top loosely with foil if it begins to dry out. Transfer the pan to a rack and arrange the olives on top. Brush the tart edges with more olive oil and let cool for about 10 minutes. Carefully remove the pan sides and slide the tart onto a cutting board. Cut into wedges and serve warm.

serves six | per serving: calories 367 (kilojoules 1,541), protein 9 g, carbohydrates 48 g, total fat 18 g, saturated fat 2 g, cholesterol 2 mg, sodium 1,531 mg, dietary fiber 4 g

shrimp bisque with chipotle cream

The smoky, earthy flavor of chipotle chiles goes well with this classic bisque. If unavailable, use 3 or 4 dry-packed sun-dried tomatoes in their place, proceeding as directed for the chiles.

2 dried chipotle chiles

boiling water, as needed

1½ lb (750 g) shrimp (prawns) in their shells with heads intact

2 yellow onions

1 large tomato, chopped

1 carrot, peeled and chopped

5 cups (40 fl oz/1.25 l) water

1 cup (8 fl oz/250 ml) dry white wine

1 fresh thyme sprig

6–8 peppercorns

¼ cup (2 oz/60 g) white rice

½ teaspoon salt

1½ cups (12 fl oz/375 ml) half-and-half (half cream)

Hungarian hot paprika or cayenne pepper to taste

pinch of coarse salt

¾ cup (6 fl oz/180 ml) sour cream

Place the chipotle chiles in a small bowl and add boiling water to cover. Set aside to soften, about 20 minutes.

Peel and devein the shrimp, reserving the shells and heads. Refrigerate the shrimp meats. Place the shells and heads in a large saucepan. Chop 1 of the onions and add to the saucepan with the tomato, carrot, water, wine, thyme, and peppercorns. Bring to a boil, reduce the heat to low, and simmer for 30 minutes. Strain through a fine-mesh sieve into a clean saucepan.

Finely chop the remaining onion and add it to the stock along with the rice and ½ teaspoon salt. Bring to a boil and cook until the rice is very tender, about 20 minutes. Let cool slightly, then, working in batches, transfer to a blender and purée until smooth. Return the purée to the saucepan. Cut the shrimp meats in half lengthwise, add to the pan, and warm over medium-low heat until cooked through, 2–3 minutes. Pour in the half-and-half and add paprika or cayenne to taste. Heat gently but do not allow to boil.

Drain the chiles, discard the stems and seeds, and place on a cutting board. Sprinkle with the coarse salt and chop to form a thick paste. In a bowl, stir together the chipotle paste and sour cream. Ladle the hot bisque into warmed bowls. Top each with a dollop of the chipotle cream and serve.

serves six | per serving: calories 302 (kilojoules 1,268), protein 23 g, carbohydrates 19 g, total fat 15 g, saturated fat 8 g, cholesterol 175 mg, sodium 393 mg, dietary fiber 2 g

sicilian orange, olive, and onion salad

Sicily, land of citrus fruit and olives, is the inspiration for this unusual salad. Blood oranges or tangerines would be welcome substitutions.

for the dressing:

1 teaspoon Dijon mustard

½ teaspoon salt

¼ teaspoon ground pepper

1 tablespoon balsamic vinegar

1 tablespoon orange juice

about ½ cup (4 fl oz/125 ml)
   extra-virgin olive oil

for the salad:

2 navel oranges

1 small red (Spanish) onion, halved
   and thinly sliced

12 oil-cured black olives, halved,
   pitted, and cut into thin slivers

8 cups (½ lb/250 g) loosely packed
   assorted young lettuce leaves

To make the dressing, in a salad bowl, whisk together the mustard, salt, pepper, vinegar, and orange juice until the salt dissolves. Slowly add the oil, whisking constantly until thickened and emulsified. Add just enough to make the dressing shiny. You should have ½ cup (4 fl oz/125 ml) dressing.

To make the salad, cut a slice off the top and bottom of each orange to expose the flesh. Place upright on a cutting board and thickly slice off the peel in strips, cutting around the contour of the orange to expose the flesh. Cut along both sides of each section to free the sections from the membranes.

Add the onion to the salad bowl and toss to separate and to coat with the dressing. Add the orange sections and the olives and toss again. Pile the lettuce greens on top. Toss the salad one more time just before serving.

serves six | per serving: calories 215 (kilojoules 903), protein 2 g, carbohydrates 9 g,
total fat 21 g, saturated fat 3 g, cholesterol 0 mg, sodium 386 mg, dietary fiber 2 g

tropical fruit salad with honey-lime dressing

This mix of exotic fruits makes a wonderful first-course dinner salad. Or accompany it with thinly sliced prosciutto and crusty bread for a poolside lunch.

for the honey-lime dressing:

2 tablespoons lime juice

1 tablespoon honey

1 teaspoon Dijon mustard

¼ teaspoon salt

⅛ teaspoon ground white pepper

¼ cup (2 fl oz/60 ml) vegetable oil

for the salad:

1 cantaloupe

1 small papaya

2 mangoes

2 kiwifruits

zest of 1 lemon, cut into long
   julienne

zest of 1 lime, cut into long julienne

To make the dressing, in a small bowl, whisk together the lime juice, honey, mustard, salt, and white pepper until the honey dissolves. Add the oil in a slow, steady stream, whisking constantly until the dressing is thick and emulsified. You should have about ½ cup (4 fl oz/125 ml). Cover and chill until serving.

To make the salad, halve and seed the cantaloupe and the papaya. Using a melon baller, form attractive rounds of the flesh of each. Alternatively, peel and cut the flesh into small cubes. Peel the mangoes and cut the flesh into 1-inch (2.5-cm) cubes. Peel the kiwifruits, cut in half lengthwise, and slice thickly. Combine all the fruits in a large bowl, cover, and chill well, at least 2 hours.

Just before serving, pour the dressing over the fruit and stir gently to coat. Spoon into a chilled glass bowl, garnish with the lemon and lime julienne, and serve immediately.

serves six | per serving: calories 205 (kilojoules 861), protein 2 g, carbohydrates 31 g, total fat 10 g, saturated fat 1 g, cholesterol 0 mg, sodium 129 mg, dietary fiber 3 g

roasted yellow pepper soup with basil swirl

for the soup:

6 large yellow bell peppers (capsicums), about 3 lb (1.5 kg) total weight

2 tablespoons plus ⅓ cup (3 fl oz/ 80 ml) olive oil

1 large yellow onion, finely chopped

1 celery stalk, thinly sliced

2 tablespoons all-purpose (plain) flour

1 lb (500 g) yellow tomatoes, peeled, seeded, and chopped

1¾ cups (14 fl oz/440 ml) chicken broth

salt and ground white pepper to taste

for the basil swirl:

2 cups (2 oz/60 g) loosely packed fresh basil leaves

1 tablespoon lemon juice

¼ cup (2 fl oz/60 ml) ice water

To make the soup, preheat a broiler (griller). Cut the peppers in half lengthwise and remove the stems, seeds, and ribs. Place, cut sides down, on a large baking sheet and broil (grill) until the skins blacken and blister. Remove from the broiler, drape with aluminum foil, let stand for 10 minutes, then peel away the skins. Cut lengthwise into narrow strips.

In a large frying pan over medium-high heat, warm the 2 tablespoons oil. Add the onion and celery and sauté until tender, about 5 minutes. Stir in the flour and cook, stirring, for 3 minutes longer. Add the peppers, tomatoes, and broth, raise the heat to high, and bring to a boil. Season with salt and white pepper. Reduce the heat to medium-high and cook uncovered, stirring often, until slightly thickened, about 15 minutes. Remove from the heat.

Let cool slightly and, working in batches, transfer to a blender. With the motor running, pour in the ⅓ cup (3 fl oz/80 ml) oil. Blend until very smooth, then strain through a fine-mesh sieve placed over a bowl. Cover and chill.

To make the basil swirl, in a blender, combine the basil and lemon juice. With the motor running, slowly pour in the water, blending until smooth.

Ladle the soup into chilled bowls. Working quickly, spoon the basil mixture into a piping bag fitted with a ⅛-inch (3-mm) tip and, starting at the center, pipe a rough spiral onto the surface of each serving. Draw a knife tip from the spiral center to the outside, forming a pattern. Serve at once.

serves six | per serving: calories 247 (kilojoules 1,037), protein 4 g, carbohydrates 21 g, total fat 18 g, saturated fat 2 g, cholesterol 0 mg, sodium 309 mg, dietary fiber 5 g

pasta salad with grilled tuna and roasted tomatoes

Serve this lunch salad to a hungry crowd just back from the beach. The ingredients can be prepared ahead of time and tossed with the dressing just before serving.

8 plum tomatoes, about 1¼ lb (625 g)
  total weight, halved lengthwise
2 tablespoons plus ½ cup
  (4 fl oz/125 ml) olive oil
salt and ground pepper to taste
1 lb (500 g) pasta shells
2 lb (1 kg) tuna fillets, about ¾ inch
  (2 cm) thick

1 cup (1 oz/30 g) loosely packed
  fresh basil leaves
3 tablespoons red wine vinegar
1 lb (500 g) fresh mozzarella cheese,
  finely diced
¼ cup (⅓ oz/10 g) chopped fresh parsley

Preheat an oven to 450°F (230°C). Prepare a hot fire in a grill.

Place the tomatoes on a baking sheet and toss with 1 tablespoon of the oil. Arrange them, cut sides up, on the sheet and sprinkle with salt. Roast until tender, about 20 minutes. Let cool, then cut in half crosswise.

Meanwhile, bring a large pot three-fourths full of salted water to a boil. Add the pasta and cook until al dente (tender but firm to the bite), about 10 minutes. Drain, rinse under cold running water, and drain again. Set aside.

Coat both sides of the tuna steaks with 1 tablespoon of the oil. Season well with salt and pepper. Place on the grill rack about 4–6 inches (10–15 cm) above the fire and grill until lightly browned, about 3 minutes. Turn and cook until done to your taste, 3–4 minutes for medium. Transfer to a cutting board, let cool, and cut into ¾-inch (2-cm) cubes.

In a food processor or blender, combine the basil leaves and the remaining ½ cup (4 fl oz/125 ml) oil. Pulse or blend until chopped to a coarse purée. Add the vinegar and season with salt and pepper. Pulse or blend until combined.

In a large bowl, combine the pasta, tomatoes and any accumulated juices, tuna, mozzarella, parsley, and basil dressing. Toss gently and serve.

serves eight | per serving: calories 700 (kilojoules 2,940), protein 44 g, carbohydrates 48 g, total fat 36 g, saturated fat 4 g, cholesterol 83 mg, sodium 289 mg, dietary fiber 2 g

roasted eggplant dip with tomato and herbs

Trim a variety of seasonal vegetables into different sizes and shapes for dipping. Carrots, celery, cucumbers, Belgian endive (chicory/witloof) leaves, radishes, zucchini (courgettes), and yellow squashes are particularly good choices. Or spread this aromatic dip on toasted slices of day-old crusty bread rubbed with garlic.

2 eggplants (aubergines), halved lengthwise and flesh scored

¼ cup (2 fl oz/60 ml) plus 2 table-spoons olive oil

salt and ground pepper to taste

2 tomatoes, peeled, seeded, and chopped

1 yellow onion, finely chopped

1 clove garlic, minced

¼ cup (⅓ oz/10 g) finely chopped mixed fresh herbs such as parsley, basil, thyme, oregano, marjoram, and chervil, in any combination

Preheat an oven to 375°F (190°C). Place the eggplants, cut sides up, in a large roasting pan. Drizzle the ¼ cup (2 fl oz/60 ml) oil over the tops and season with salt and pepper. Bake until soft and tender, 30–40 minutes. Remove from the oven and, when cool enough to handle, use a large spoon to scoop out the cooked flesh. Discard the skins and finely chop the flesh.

In a bowl, combine the chopped eggplant, tomatoes, onion, and garlic. Stir in the 2 tablespoons oil and season with salt and pepper. (The dip can be made up to 2 days in advance. Cover and refrigerate.)

Just before serving, stir in the herbs, then taste and adjust the seasonings.

serves six | per serving: calories 172 (kilojoules 722), protein 2 g, carbohydrates 12 g, total fat 14 g, saturated fat 2 g, cholesterol 0 mg, sodium 10 mg, dietary fiber 3 g

main dishes

new england stove-top clambake

Here is an easy way to re-create a traditional Native American feast. For best results, look for a large, industrial stockpot in a restaurant-supply house.

2 lb (1 kg) well-rinsed seaweed or
  corn husks, soaked in cold water
  for 1 hour and drained
3 celery stalks, coarsely chopped
12–18 small red potatoes
salt and ground pepper to taste
1 chicken, about 3½ lb (1.75 kg),
  cut into 6 serving pieces
1½ lb (750 g) kielbasa or similar
  smoked pork sausage, cut into
  6 equal pieces

6 small yellow onions
6 small lobsters, scrubbed clean
6 ears of corn, shucked
4 dozen soft-shell clams such as
  steamers or razor clams
2 dozen mussels, well scrubbed
  and debearded
1 cup (8 oz/250 g) unsalted butter,
  melted
2 lemons, cut into wedges

Line the bottom of a very large stockpot with the seaweed or corn husks. Add the celery and cold water to cover (about 6 cups/48 fl oz/1.5 l). Bring to a boil over medium-high heat. Add the potatoes, then reduce the heat to medium, season with salt and pepper, and cook for 15 minutes.

Meanwhile, cut 6 pieces of cheesecloth (muslin) each 18 by 36 inches (45 by 90 cm). Divide the chicken and sausage evenly among the cheesecloth pieces and wrap well. Place the onions and then the chicken-sausage packets on top of the potatoes, season with salt and pepper, cover, and cook for 15 minutes. Add the lobsters and corn, again season with salt and pepper, re-cover, and cook for 8 minutes. Place the clams and mussels in the pot, discarding any that do not close to the touch, and cover. Cook until the shells open, about 10 minutes.

Uncover and discard any clams and mussels that did not open. Ladle the clams and mussels into large bowls and spoon over some of the cooking liquid from the pot. Serve as a first course. Serve the potatoes, onions, chicken, sausage, lobster, and corn on large individual plates as the main course. Accompany with the melted butter and lemon wedges.

serves six | per serving: calories 1,610 (kilojoules 6,762), protein 100 g, carbohydrates 97 g, total fat 94 g, saturated fat 39 g, cholesterol 413 mg, sodium 1,953 mg, dietary fiber 12 g

cumin-rubbed lamb skewers with roasted peppers

Toast and grind whole cumin seeds to give the lamb the full effect of this pungent spice. Serve with couscous tossed with an assortment of finely chopped fresh herbs and sautéed cherry tomatoes.

2 lb (1 kg) lean lamb, preferably
  cut from the leg

2 tablespoons ground cumin

2 teaspoons salt

½ teaspoon ground pepper

4 tablespoons (2 fl oz/60 ml)
  olive oil

2 red bell peppers (capsicums)

2 yellow bell peppers (capsicums)

16 mushrooms, about ½ lb (250 g)
  total weight, brushed clean, stems
  trimmed, and caps halved

Cut the lamb into sixteen 2½–3-inch (6–7.5-cm) cubes. Place in a large bowl and sprinkle with the cumin, salt, and pepper. Using your hands, rub the cumin mixture into the lamb cubes. Add 2 tablespoons of the olive oil, toss well to coat, cover, and refrigerate for 12–24 hours.

Preheat a broiler (griller). Cut the bell peppers in half lengthwise and discard the stems, seeds, and ribs. Place, cut sides down, on a baking sheet and broil (grill) until the skins blacken and blister. Remove from the broiler, drape loosely with aluminum foil, let stand for 10 minutes, then peel away the skins. Cut lengthwise into wide strips; you will need 32 strips.

Prepare a medium-hot fire in a grill, or leave the broiler on.

Thread the lamb cubes onto 8 long metal skewers, dividing evenly and alternating them with the pepper strips and mushroom halves.

Brush the skewers with the remaining 2 tablespoons olive oil. Place on the grill rack or under a broiler about 6 inches (15 cm) from the heat source. Grill or broil, turning often, until the lamb is well browned and firm to the touch, 12–15 minutes for medium. Transfer to individual plates and serve at once.

serves four | per serving: calories 475 (kilojoules 1,995), protein 51 g, carbohydrates 9 g, total fat 26 g, saturated fat 6 g, cholesterol 152 mg, sodium 1,290 mg, dietary fiber 2 g

lime-and-coconut-soaked chicken with cilantro

The tropical flavors of lime and coconut add an extra exotic touch to this simple dish. If you like, add one lemongrass stalk (tender base only), chopped, and/or one 2-inch (5-cm) piece fresh ginger, peeled and grated, to the marinade. Serve the skewers on a bed of rice or couscous.

1¼ cups (14 fl oz/430 ml) canned coconut milk

⅓ cup (3 fl oz/80 ml) lime juice

1½ lb (750 g) boneless, skinless chicken breasts, cut into 1-inch (2.5-cm) cubes

salt and ground pepper to taste

2 tablespoons finely chopped fresh cilantro (fresh coriander)

In a large bowl, stir together the coconut milk and lime juice. Add the chicken, turn to coat, and refrigerate for 4 hours or for up to overnight.

Prepare a medium-hot fire in a grill, or preheat a broiler (griller).

Remove the chicken from the marinade and pat dry with paper towels. Thread the cubes of chicken onto 4 long metal skewers. Season well with salt and pepper. Place the skewers on the grill rack or under a broiler about 5–6 inches (13–15 cm) from the heat source. Grill or broil, turning often, until lightly browned and no longer pink in the center when cut into with a sharp knife, 7–10 minutes.

Remove from the grill or broiler, sprinkle evenly with the cilantro, and serve immediately.

serves four | per serving: calories 216 (kilojouoles 907), protein 40 g, carbohydrates 1 g, total fat 5 g, saturated fat 3 g, cholesterol 99 mg, sodium 113 mg, dietary fiber 0 g

fish cakes with coriander

A quick tomato sauce or spicy tomato salsa, tartar sauce,
or lemon wedges would complement these fish cakes.

2 tablespoons olive oil

½ cup (2½ oz/75 g) finely chopped
  red bell pepper (capsicum)

½ cup (2½ oz/75 g) finely chopped
  green bell pepper (capsicum)

1 yellow onion, finely chopped

1 tablespoon finely chopped fresh
  thyme

salt to taste, plus 1 teaspoon

ground pepper to taste,
  plus ½ teaspoon

2 lb (1 kg) cod fillets, trimmed of
  skin and any errant bones
  removed, cut into large pieces

1 cup (2 oz/60 g) fresh bread
  crumbs

2 tablespoons coriander seeds

vegetable oil for frying

1 cup (5 oz/155 g) all-purpose
  (plain) flour

In a small saucepan over medium-high heat, warm the olive oil. Add the
bell peppers and onion and sauté until softened, 7–10 minutes. Stir in the
thyme and season to taste with salt and pepper. Let cool.

Line a baking sheet with waxed paper. In a food processor, working in
batches, process the cod until ground, 20–30 seconds per batch. Transfer to
a bowl. Add the pepper mixture, bread crumbs, 1 teaspoon salt, and ½ teaspoon pepper. Stir just until the mixture holds together loosely. Divide into 12
equal portions and form into cakes about 2½ inches (6 cm) in diameter. Place
on the prepared baking sheet, cover tightly, and refrigerate for at least 2 hours
or for up to 12 hours.

In a small, dry frying pan over medium heat, toast the coriander seeds,
shaking the pan often, until fragrant and lightly browned, 3–5 minutes. Let
cool slightly, then crush lightly.

In a large, heavy frying pan over medium-high heat, pour in oil to a
depth of ¼ inch (6 mm). Heat until hot but not smoking. Dredge the cakes
in the flour and tap off excess. Working in batches, fry, turning once, until
golden brown and firm to the touch, 3–5 minutes on each side. Transfer to
paper towels to drain and season with salt and pepper; keep warm.

Sprinkle the cakes with the coriander seeds and serve immediately.

serves six | per serving: calories 483 (kilojoules 2,029), protein 33 g, carbohydrates 42 g,
total fat 21 g, saturated fat 3 g, cholesterol 65 mg, sodium 563 mg, dietary fiber 6 g

honey-glazed salmon with roasted corn salsa

for the salsa:

3 ears of corn, shucked

2 tomatoes, peeled, seeded, and
  chopped

1 small yellow onion, finely
  chopped

2 tablespoons olive oil

1 tablespoon red wine vinegar

½ teaspoon salt

¼ teaspoon ground pepper

¼ teaspoon Tabasco or other hot-
  pepper sauce, or to taste

2 tablespoons finely chopped fresh
  parsley

for the salmon:

½ cup (6 oz/185 g) honey

2 tablespoons balsamic vinegar

1 tablespoon plus 2 teaspoons
  vegetable oil

6 center-cut salmon fillets with skin
  intact, 6–8 oz (185–250 g) each

salt and ground pepper to taste

To make the salsa, prepare a hot fire in a grill. Place the corn on the grill rack 5–6 inches (13–15 cm) from the fire and cook, turning often, until the kernels have softened and are lightly browned, about 10 minutes. Let cool completely, then cut off the kernels from each ear with a sharp knife, cutting the length of the ear and rotating it with each cut.

In a large bowl, combine the corn kernels, tomatoes, onion, oil, vinegar, salt, pepper, and hot-pepper sauce. Stir well, then taste and adjust the seasonings. Cover and refrigerate. Stir in the parsley just before serving.

To prepare the salmon, in a small saucepan, stir together the honey, vinegar, and the 1 tablespoon oil. Bring to a boil over high heat, reduce the heat to medium-low, and cook, stirring often, until reduced by half, 2–3 minutes.

In a heavy, large nonstick frying pan over medium-high heat, warm the 2 teaspoons oil. Season the salmon with salt and pepper and place skin side down in the pan. Brush the tops generously with the honey mixture and cook for 5 minutes. Turn over the salmon and brush again with the honey mixture. Cook, turning occasionally and brushing with the honey mixture, until the salmon is glazed and opaque throughout, 5–7 minutes longer. Transfer to warmed individual plates. Pass the salsa at the table.

serves six | per serving: calories 602 (kilojoules 2,528), protein 42 g, carbohydrates 41 g, total fat 31 g, saturated fat 6 g, cholesterol 117 mg, sodium 328 mg, dietary fiber 3 g

raw bar with three dipping sauces

Fill large roasting pans or glass baking dishes with shaved or finely cracked ice. Arrange on top an assortment of oysters and clams on the half shell. Serve with the following dipping sauces in bowls on the side.

4 dozen oysters on the half shell
8 dozen clams on the half shell

for sauce one:
1 cup (8 oz/250 g) plain yogurt
1 red bell pepper (capsicum), roasted, peeled, and chopped (see method page 59)
3 or 4 dry-packed sun-dried tomatoes, softened in warm water for 20 minutes and drained
1 tablespoon olive oil
1 tablespoon balsamic vinegar
½ small fresh chile, seeded and minced
1 small clove garlic, minced

for sauce two:
1 cup (6 oz/185 g) peeled and diced papaya

½ cup (3 oz/90 g) peeled and diced mango
1 piece fresh ginger, 2 inches (5 cm) long, peeled and grated
½ small fresh chile, seeded and minced
½ cup (½ oz/15 g) loosely packed fresh mint leaves
2 tablespoons lime juice

for sauce three:
2 tablespoons Southeast Asian fish sauce
2 tablespoons lime juice
2 large wedges ripe tomato
1 tablespoon dark brown sugar
½ cup (2½ oz/75 g) salted roasted peanuts
1 cup (1 oz/30 g) loosely packed fresh cilantro (fresh coriander) leaves

To make each sauce, combine all its ingredients in a food processor or blender and process until smooth. Transfer to separate bowls and chill for at least 2 hours. The sauces can be made up to 1 day in advance.

serves four | per serving: calories 640 (kilojoules 2,688), protein 68 g, carbohydrates 42 g, total fat 22 g, saturated fat 4 g, cholesterol 219 mg, sodium 887 mg, dietary fiber 4 g

grilled pork medallions with curried peach salsa

2 tablespoons soy sauce

2 tablespoons red wine vinegar

2 tablespoons olive oil

1 tablespoon chopped fresh thyme

1½ lb (750 g) pork tenderloin, cut
   crosswise into slices 2 inches
   (5 cm) thick and lightly pounded

salt and ground pepper to taste

for the salsa:

2 tablespoons unsalted butter

1 small yellow onion, finely chopped

1 celery stalk, finely chopped

2 teaspoons mild curry powder, or
   more to taste

½ cup (4 fl oz/125 ml) water

6 small peaches, peeled, pitted, and
   cut into ½-inch (12-mm) dice

1 small red bell pepper (capsicum),
   seeded and cut into ¼-inch
   (6-mm) dice

½ cup (¾ oz/20 g) finely chopped
   fresh cilantro (fresh coriander)

salt and ground pepper to taste

In a small bowl, stir together the soy sauce, vinegar, oil, and thyme. Place the pork medallions in a shallow dish and pour over the soy mixture. Cover and refrigerate, turning often, for 3 hours or up to overnight.

Meanwhile, make the salsa: In a small saucepan over medium-high heat, melt the butter. Add the onion and celery and sauté until softened, about 5 minutes. Stir in the curry powder and cook, stirring often, until well blended, about 2 minutes longer. Remove from the heat and pour in the water. Stir well to blend, cover, and let cool to room temperature.

In a bowl, combine the peaches, bell pepper, and curry mixture. Stir well, cover, and refrigerate. Just before serving, stir in the cilantro and season with salt and pepper.

Prepare a medium-hot fire in a grill, or preheat a broiler (griller). Remove the pork from the marinade and pat dry. Season with salt and pepper. Place on the grill rack or under the broiler 4–6 inches (10–15 cm) from the heat source. Grill or broil, turning once, until lightly browned on the outside and slightly pink when cut into the center, about 5 minutes on each side.

Transfer to warmed individual plates. Pass the salsa at the table.

serves four | per serving: calories 398 (kilojoules 1,672), protein 36 g, carbohydrates 21 g, total fat 19 g, saturated fat 7 g, cholesterol 123 mg, sodium 343 mg, dietary fiber 4 g

blt wraps with tahini sauce

These are the perfect sandwiches to tote on a boat for a portable lunch. Lavash, Armenian cracker bread available in both soft and crisp forms, is available in Middle Eastern markets and in well-stocked food stores. If unavailable, use pita bread split in half horizontally.

½ cup (5 oz/155 g) tahini
  (sesame paste)
2 tablespoons olive oil
2 tablespoons soy sauce
2 tablespoons white wine vinegar
  or rice vinegar
¼ teaspoon red pepper flakes

¼ lb (125 g) thinly sliced bacon
2 large soft lavash, each about
  16 inches (40 cm) in diameter
2 large tomatoes, thinly sliced
1 large head romaine (cos) lettuce,
  leaves separated and cut into
  coarse strips

In a small bowl, stir together the tahini, oil, soy sauce, vinegar, and pepper flakes until smooth.

In a large frying pan over medium-high heat, fry the bacon until browned and crisp, about 5 minutes. Transfer to paper towels to drain.

Cut each bread round into quarters. Spread each quarter with an equal amount of the tahini mixture. Break the bacon into large pieces and scatter over the quarters. Top with the tomato slices and then the lettuce strips. Working with 1 quarter at a time, fold the point about one-third of the way toward the rounded edge, then roll up left to right into a tight log. Wrap each quarter securely in parchment (baking) or waxed paper. Cut off any excess paper. The wraps are now ready to be "peeled" and eaten.

serves four | per serving: calories 625 (kilojoules 2,625), protein 24 g, carbohydrates 70 g, total fat 30 g, saturated fat 5 g, cholesterol 7 mg, sodium 867 mg, dietary fiber 12 g

soft-shell crab sandwiches

for the pesto mayonnaise:

1 cup (1½ oz/45 g) tightly packed fresh basil leaves

5 cloves garlic, coarsely chopped

½ cup (2½ oz/75 g) pine nuts, toasted

¾ cup (6 fl oz/180 ml) olive oil

1 cup (8 fl oz/250 ml) mayonnaise

salt and ground pepper to taste

for the soft-shell crabs:

12 small soft-shell crabs

1 cup (5 oz/155 g) all-purpose (plain) flour

1 teaspoon salt

½ teaspoon ground pepper

¼ teaspoon paprika

6 tablespoons (3 oz/90 g) unsalted butter

for the sandwiches:

6 large rolls, preferably brioche, split and toasted

2 large tomatoes, peeled, seeded, and cut into ¼-inch (6-mm) dice

6 large lettuce leaves

salt and ground pepper to taste

To make the mayonnaise, in a food processor or blender, combine the basil, garlic, and pine nuts. Process briefly to mix. With the motor running, slowly pour in the oil and process until thick, about 30 seconds. Transfer to a bowl and stir in the mayonnaise. Season with salt and pepper. Cover and refrigerate until ready to assemble the sandwiches.

First, clean the soft-shell crabs: Working with one at a time, turn it on its back and lift up and snap off the apron. Lift the flaps on either end of the body and pull out and discard the spongy gill tissue. Snip away the eyes, then discard the bile sac near the top of the legs. Dry thoroughly.

In a shallow bowl, combine the flour, salt, pepper, and paprika. Coat the crabs lightly in the mixture, tapping off any excess. In a large frying pan over medium-high heat, melt half of the butter until sizzling. Add 6 crabs and cook, turning once, until browned, about 3 minutes on each side. Keep warm on a plate. Repeat with the remaining butter and crabs.

Liberally spread the cut sides of the rolls with the mayonnaise. Place 2 crabs on the bottom of each roll and top with the tomato and lettuce. Season with salt and pepper, place the tops on, and serve immediately.

serves six | per serving: calories 1,090 (kilojoules 4,578), protein 28 g, carbohydrates 66 g, total fat 82 g, saturated fat 18 g, cholesterol 214 mg, sodium 1,516 mg, dietary fiber 5 g

grilled swordfish steaks with ginger-orange butter

A compound butter is a great way to dress up any grilled fish.
Try creating your own butter using fresh herbs or other citrus fruits
such as lemon or lime.

for the butter:

¼ cup (2 oz/60 g) unsalted butter,
  at room temperature

1 tablespoon orange juice

1 piece fresh ginger, 3 inches
  (7.5 cm) long, peeled and grated

1 teaspoon finely grated orange zest

¼ teaspoon salt

¼ teaspoon white pepper

1 tablespoon snipped fresh chives

for the fish:

4 swordfish steaks, each about 6 oz
  (185 g) and 1 inch (2.5 cm) thick

salt and ground pepper to taste

¼ cup (2 fl oz/60 ml) orange juice

2 tablespoons olive oil

To make the butter, in a food processor, combine the butter, orange juice, ginger, orange zest, salt, and white pepper and process until blended. Add the chives and process briefly to mix. Alternatively, mix together in a small bowl with a wooden spoon. Place the butter on a piece of plastic wrap and shape into a cylinder 4 inches (10 cm) long. Wrap securely and refrigerate until serving. (The butter can be made and refrigerated up to 2 days in advance or frozen for up to 2 months.)

Season the fish with salt and pepper. Place in a nonreactive baking dish and pour the orange juice and olive oil over the top. Cover and refrigerate for 1 hour, turning several times.

Prepare a hot fire in a grill, or preheat a broiler (griller). Remove the fish from the marinade and pat dry with paper towels. Place on the grill rack or under the broiler 5–6 inches (13–15 cm) from the heat source. Grill or broil, turning once, until lightly browned and opaque throughout, about 5 minutes on each side.

Transfer the fish steaks to warmed individual plates. Cut the butter into 4 equal pieces and place on the steaks. Serve at once.

serves four | per serving: calories 307 (kilojoules 1,289), protein 30 g, carbohydrates 2 g, total fat 19 g, saturated fat 9 g, cholesterol 90 mg, sodium 282 mg, dietary fiber 0 g

red snapper ceviche with tomatillos and chiles

Use the freshest snapper available. If tomatillos are unavailable, use seeded green tomatoes in their place.

1 lb (500 g) skinless red snapper fillet, cut into ½-inch (12-mm) dice

¾ cup (6 fl oz/180 ml) lime juice (from 6–8 limes)

4 or 5 small tomatillos, about ½ lb (250 g) total weight, husks removed and cut into ¼-inch (6-mm) dice

1 firm but ripe tomato, seeded and cut into ¼-inch (6-mm) dice

1 small jalapeño chile, seeded and minced

1 small clove garlic, minced

½ small white onion, cut into ¼-inch (6-mm) dice

¼ cup (2 fl oz/60 ml) olive oil

½ cup (¾ oz/20 g) finely chopped fresh cilantro (fresh coriander)

salt and ground pepper to taste

8 large butter (Boston) or green-leaf lettuce leaves

In a large nonaluminum bowl, combine the snapper and the lime juice, turning to coat. Cover and refrigerate for 4–6 hours.

Add the tomatillos, tomato, jalapeño, garlic, and onion to the fish and mix gently. Stir in the oil and cilantro. Season with salt and pepper.

Line a chilled shallow bowl with the lettuce leaves. Using a slotted spoon, transfer the ceviche to the center. Serve immediately.

serves four to six | per serving: calories 214 (kilojoules 899), protein 20 g, carbohydrates 6 g, total fat 12 g, saturated fat 2 g, cholesterol 34 mg, sodium 66 mg, dietary fiber 1 g

monkfish stew with fennel and olives

For a true taste of the Mediterranean, dissolve a few saffron threads in a little water and add to the stew during the last 5 minutes of cooking. Serve with crusty garlic bread.

3 tablespoons olive oil

1½ lb (750 g) skinless monkfish fillet, cut into 2-inch (5-cm) pieces

salt and ground pepper to taste

¼ cup (2½ oz/75 g) all-purpose (plain) flour

3 Yukon gold or similar firm-fleshed boiling potatoes, about 1½ lb (750 g) total weight, peeled and diced

2 large fennel bulbs, trimmed and thinly sliced

1 yellow onion, thinly sliced

2 cups (16 fl oz/500 ml) fish stock

½ cup (4 fl oz/125 ml) dry white wine

2 tomatoes, peeled, seeded, and chopped

1 tablespoon finely chopped fresh thyme

¼ cup (2½ oz/75 g) pitted black olives, coarsely chopped

1 tablespoon finely chopped fresh flat-leaf (Italian) parsley

In a large, deep frying pan over medium-high heat, warm 2 tablespoons of the oil. Pat the fish dry with paper towels, season well with salt and pepper, and then coat with the flour, tapping off any excess. Place in the pan and cook, turning often, until lightly browned on all sides, 5–7 minutes. Transfer to paper towels to drain.

Add the remaining 1 tablespoon oil to the pan along with the potatoes, fennel, and onion. Season with salt and pepper. Cover partially and cook, stirring often, until the fennel has wilted and the potatoes are slightly softened, about 10 minutes. Add the stock, wine, tomatoes, and thyme, raise the heat slightly, and cook uncovered, stirring often, until slightly thickened and the potatoes are tender, about 15 minutes. Add the olives, browned fish, and parsley, and cook until the fish is opaque throughout, 5–7 minutes longer. Season with salt and pepper.

Transfer to a warmed serving dish and serve very hot.

serves four to six | per serving: calories 407 (kilojoules 1,709), protein 26 g, carbohydrates 43 g, total fat 12 g, saturated fat 1 g, cholesterol 34 mg, sodium 413 mg, dietary fiber 6 g

jambalaya

Frozen cooked crayfish are found in well-stocked food stores; if unavailable, omit them and increase the shrimp to 1½ pounds (750 g).

2 tablespoons vegetable oil, or
  as needed

¾ lb (375 g) andouille sausage or
  similar smoked spicy sausage,
  thinly sliced

1 large yellow onion, finely chopped

2 celery stalks, thinly sliced

2 green bell peppers (capsicums),
  seeded and finely chopped

3 cloves garlic, minced

1 teaspoon dried oregano

1 teaspoon dried thyme

1 teaspoon paprika

¼ teaspoon cayenne pepper

2 bay leaves

salt and ground pepper to taste

2 cups (14 oz/440 g) long-grain
  white rice

3⅓ cups (27 fl oz/830 ml) chicken
  broth

1 can (15 oz/470 g) crushed
  tomatoes in thick purée

1 lb (500 g) shrimp (prawns),
  peeled and deveined

1 lb (500 g) cooked crayfish
  (see note)

3 green (spring) onions, including
  tender green tops, chopped

In a large pot over medium-high heat, warm the 2 tablespoons oil. Add the sausage and cook, stirring often, until golden brown, about 5 minutes. Using a slotted spoon, transfer to a plate. Pour off all but 2 tablespoons fat from the pot; if less remains, add enough oil to make 2 tablespoons.

Return the pot to medium-high heat and add the onion, celery, bell peppers, and garlic. Cover and cook, stirring often, until the vegetables start to soften, about 5 minutes. Stir in the oregano, thyme, paprika, cayenne, and bay leaves. Season with salt and pepper. Add the rice and cook, stirring, for 1 minute. Add the broth and tomatoes, cover, and bring to a boil. Reduce the heat to low and simmer until the rice is almost done, about 15 minutes.

Raise the heat to medium and stir in the reserved sausage and the shrimp. Set the crayfish on top. Bring back to a simmer, cover, and cook for 3 minutes. Remove from the heat and let stand, covered, until the rice and shrimp are just done, about 5 minutes. Then uncover, remove the crayfish, and stir in the green onions. Spoon into a warmed serving dish, arrange the crayfish on top, and serve.

serves six | per serving: calories 705 (kilojoules 2,961), protein 49 g, carbohydrates 65 g, total fat 26 g, saturated fat 7 g, cholesterol 275 mg, sodium 1,562 mg, dietary fiber 2 g

panfried tuna with black bean salsa

Goya brand canned black beans are best for the salsa, as they are firm and hold their shape better than most other brands. If the salsa needs more heat, reserve seeds from the chile and add to taste just before serving.

for the black bean salsa:

2 cans (15 oz/470 g each) black beans, drained and rinsed (see note)

3 tomatoes, seeded and finely diced

1 red (Spanish) onion, finely chopped

½ cup (¾ oz/20 g) finely chopped fresh cilantro (fresh coriander)

¼ cup (⅓ oz/10 g) finely chopped fresh parsley

1 jalapeño chile, seeded and minced

½ cup (4 fl oz/125 ml) tomato juice

3½ tablespoons lime juice (about 2 limes)

salt and ground pepper to taste

6 tuna steaks, each about 6 oz (185 g) and 1 inch (2.5 cm) thick

¼ cup (2 fl oz/60 ml) olive oil

salt and ground pepper to taste

To make the salsa, in a large bowl, combine the beans, tomatoes, onion, cilantro, parsley, chile, tomato juice, and lime juice. Stir well and season with salt and pepper. Cover and chill for about 15 minutes.

Preheat a large frying pan or stove-top grill pan over medium-high heat. Coat the tuna with the oil and season with salt and pepper. Place the tuna in the pan and cook until golden brown on the underside, about 2½ minutes. Turn and cook until golden brown on the second side and done to your liking, about 2½ minutes longer for medium-rare.

Transfer to warmed individual plates and serve immediately. Pass the salsa at the table.

serves six | per serving: calories 412 (kilojoules 1,730), protein 42 g, carbohydrates 21 g, total fat 17 g, saturated fat 3 g, cholesterol 58 mg, sodium 373 mg, dietary fiber 6 g

jerked chicken grilled under a brick

There is a wide range given here for the chiles. In Jamaica, where jerk originated, most cooks would use the maximum amount. The minimum amount is tame but still spicy. Weighting the chicken pieces as they grill helps them cook evenly and keeps them moist.

4–8 very hot fresh chiles such as Scotch bonnet or habanero, seeded (see note)

4 green (spring) onions, including tender green tops, chopped

juice of 1 orange

juice of 2 limes

2 tablespoons mixed dried herbs such as thyme, rosemary, and oregano, in any combination

1 tablespoon distilled white or cider vinegar

1 tablespoon ground allspice

1 tablespoon ground coriander

1 tablespoon dry hot mustard

1 tablespoon coarse salt

1 tablespoon ground pepper

6 chicken legs (thigh and drumstick), about ½ lb (250 g) each

Prepare a medium-hot fire in a grill. Wrap 6 bricks or flat rocks in aluminum foil.

In a food processor or blender, combine the chiles, green onions, orange juice, lime juice, dried herbs, vinegar, allspice, coriander, mustard, salt, and pepper. Process to a paste. Smear the chicken pieces with the paste.

Place the chicken pieces on the grill rack 5–6 inches (13–15 cm) from the fire and top each piece with a brick. (The fire must not be too hot or the outside of the chicken will be charred and the inside will remain raw.) Grill until nicely browned on the underside, about 15 minutes. Remove the bricks, turn the pieces over, and replace the bricks. Continue to grill until nicely browned on the second side and no longer pink in the center when cut into with a knife, about 15 minutes longer.

Transfer to a large platter and serve warm or at room temperature.

serves six | per serving: calories 289 (kilojoules 1,214), protein 30 g, carbohydrates 6 g, total fat 16 g, saturated fat 4 g, cholesterol 103 mg, sodium 838 mg, dietary fiber 1 g

seafood quiche

for the filling:

½ lb (250 g) cooked lobster meat, cut into 1-inch (2.5-cm) pieces

½ lb (250 g) cooked lump crabmeat, picked over for shell fragments

½ lb (250 g) cooked shrimp (prawns), peeled and deveined

2 tablespoons vodka

1 tablespoon lemon juice

⅛ teaspoon cayenne pepper

4 eggs

1 cup (8 fl oz/250 ml) heavy (double) cream

½ cup (2 oz/60 g) grated Parmesan cheese

½ teaspoon salt

1 cup (1½ oz/45 g) tightly packed watercress leaves

1 tablespoon Dijon mustard

for the pastry:

1 cup (5 oz/155 g) all-purpose (plain) flour

½ cup (2½ oz/75 g) yellow cornmeal

1 teaspoon salt

¾ cup (6 oz/185 g) chilled unsalted butter, cut into small pieces

3 tablespoons ice water, or more if needed

To begin the filling, in a bowl, combine the lobster, crab, and shrimp. Sprinkle with the vodka, lemon juice, and cayenne and toss gently. Cover and refrigerate until ready to assemble the quiche.

To make the pastry, in a bowl, stir together the flour, cornmeal, and salt. Using 2 knives or a pastry blender, cut in the butter until the mixture resembles coarse crumbs. Stirring and tossing with a fork, sprinkle with enough ice water to moisten lightly. Gather the dough into a ball.

On a lightly floured surface, roll out the dough into a 12-inch (30-cm) round. Transfer to a 9-inch (23-cm) deep-dish pie pan. Trim the edges and flute attractively. Chill for 10 minutes. Preheat an oven to 375°F (190°C).

Finish the filling: In a bowl, whisk together the eggs, cream, cheese, and salt. Drain any liquid from the seafood into the egg mixture, whisk again, and stir in the watercress. Brush the bottom of the pastry shell with the mustard. Top with the seafood and then the egg mixture.

Bake until the filling is just set, about 25 minutes. Transfer to a rack. Serve warm or at room temperature.

serves six to eight | per serving: calories 595 (kilojoules 2,499), protein 31 g, carbohydrates 26 g, total fat 39 g, saturated fat 23 g, cholesterol 347 mg, sodium 1,042 mg, dietary fiber 1 g

beef tenderloin with quick ratatouille

The ratatouille can be served at room temperature. A golden brown–topped potato gratin makes a perfect side dish.

9 tablespoons (4½ fl oz/140 ml) olive oil

2 yellow onions, coarsely chopped

6 cloves garlic, minced

2 zucchini (courgettes), quartered lengthwise, seeded, and cut into chunks

1 large eggplant (aubergine), cut into cubes

2 fresh tomatoes, seeded and chopped

1 can (15 oz/470 g) crushed tomatoes in thick purée

⅓ cup (½ oz/15 g) finely chopped fresh parsley

2 tablespoons chopped fresh thyme

salt and ground pepper to taste

1 beef tenderloin, 2½ lb (1.25 kg), tied with string

In a large, heavy, wide pot over medium-high heat, warm 1 tablespoon of the oil. Add the onions and garlic and cook, stirring often, until the onions are tender, about 5 minutes. Transfer to a plate.

Heat 7 tablespoons (3½ fl oz/105 ml) of the oil in the same pot over medium-high heat. Add the zucchini and eggplant and cook, stirring often, until golden, about 10 minutes. Add the onion mixture, the fresh and canned tomatoes, the parsley, and the thyme. Season with salt and pepper. Simmer, stirring often, until slightly thickened and pulpy, about 10 minutes. Season again with salt and pepper.

Meanwhile, preheat an oven to 400°F (200°C). Put the tenderloin in a roasting pan and coat with the remaining 1 tablespoon oil. Season with salt and pepper.

Roast the tenderloin until an instant-read thermometer inserted into the thickest part registers 130°F (54°C) for medium-rare, 30–35 minutes, or until done to your liking. Transfer to a warm spot, cover loosely with aluminum foil, and let stand for 10 minutes.

Cut into slices against the grain. Arrange several slices, overlapping, on warmed plates. Spoon a small amount of the ratatouille on the side.

serves six | per serving: calories 634 (kilojoules 2,663), protein 36 g, carbohydrates 22 g, total fat 45 g, saturated fat 13 g, cholesterol 109 mg, sodium 201 mg, dietary fiber 4 g

seared scallops with saffron creamed corn

Present this elegant main course on large decorative plates that set off the special color of saffron. Serve with crumb-topped broiled tomatoes.

1 cup (8 fl oz/250 ml) heavy
   (double) cream
pinch of saffron threads
2 tablespoons olive oil
1 large carrot, peeled and finely
   chopped
1 yellow onion, finely chopped
1 celery stalk, halved lengthwise
   and thinly sliced

6 cups (2¼ lb/1.1 kg) corn kernels
   (from about 8 ears)
salt and ground pepper to taste
2 tablespoons unsalted butter
2 tablespoons vegetable oil
18 sea scallops, about 1½ lb (750 g)
   total weight
1 tablespoon finely chopped fresh
   parsley

In a small saucepan over medium-high heat, combine the cream and the saffron. Bring just to a boil, remove from the heat, cover, and let stand for 10 minutes. Stir well to infuse the cream with the saffron.

In a large, heavy frying pan over medium-high heat, warm the olive oil. Add the carrot, onion, and celery and sauté until softened, 5–7 minutes. Stir in the corn and cook, stirring occasionally, until just beginning to soften, about 5 minutes. Pour in the cream mixture and season well with salt and pepper. Cook, stirring often, until the cream thickens slightly and the corn is tender, about 10 minutes longer. (The recipe can be made up to this point 1 day in advance. Cover and refrigerate.)

Just before serving, in a large frying pan over high heat, melt the butter with the vegetable oil. Season the scallops with salt and pepper and, working in batches if necessary, place in the pan in a single layer. Do not crowd the pan. Cook, turning once, until browned on the outside and just opaque in the center, about 2 minutes on each side.

Reheat the corn if necessary, then taste and adjust the seasonings. Divide the corn evenly among warmed individual plates. Top with the scallops, sprinkle with the parsley, and serve at once.

serves six | per serving: calories 516 (kilojoules 2,167), protein 26 g, carbohydrates 41 g, total fat 30 g, saturated fat 13 g, cholesterol 102 mg, sodium 237 mg, dietary fiber 7 g

summer squash stuffed with lamb

Stuffed vegetables are easy to make ahead and then bake at the last minute. Try ground (minced) beef, veal, or turkey in place of the lamb.

3 yellow summer squashes

3 zucchini (courgettes)

ice water, to cover

3 tablespoons olive oil

1 large yellow onion, finely chopped

1 clove garlic, minced

1½ lb (750 g) ground (minced) lean lamb

2 tomatoes, peeled, seeded, and coarsely chopped

1 tablespoon tomato paste

1 teaspoon finely chopped fresh thyme

salt and ground pepper to taste

½ cup (1 oz/30 g) fresh bread crumbs

Bring a large pot three-fourths full of salted water to a boil. Halve the squashes and zucchini lengthwise. Using a small spoon, scoop out the seeds and enough flesh to form a shell ¼ inch (6 mm) thick. Add the shells to the boiling water. Boil until barely tender but not limp, about 1 minute. Using a slotted spoon, transfer the shells to a bowl of ice water. Let cool completely, then transfer to paper towels to drain.

In a large frying pan over medium-high heat, warm 2 tablespoons of the oil. Add the onion and sauté until tender, about 5 minutes. Add the garlic and sauté for about 1 minute longer. Stir in the lamb, tomatoes, tomato paste, thyme, salt, and pepper. Cook, stirring often, until the mixture thickens and the liquid has almost evaporated, about 15 minutes. Season again with salt and pepper. (The recipe can be prepared up to this point several hours in advance. Refrigerate the shells and the filling separately.)

Preheat an oven to 375°F (190°C). Line a large baking sheet with heavy-duty aluminum foil and lightly oil the foil.

Fill the shells with equal amounts of the lamb mixture and place on the prepared baking sheet. Sprinkle the bread crumbs evenly over the tops and drizzle with the remaining 1 tablespoon oil.

Bake until heated through and browned on top, 12–15 minutes. Serve hot.

serves six | per serving: calories 293 (kilojoules 1,231), protein 25 g, carbohydrates 15 g, total fat 15 g, saturated fat 4 g, cholesterol 75 mg, sodium 134 mg, dietary fiber 3 g

ancho chile–rubbed flank steaks

Quick and easy to grill, flank steak is perfect for
the beach house. Ancho chiles are dark red and have an earthy,
slightly sweet flavor. They are not blisteringly hot. Marinate the steak
overnight for a more intense flavor.

4 ancho chiles

2 cloves garlic

2 teaspoons coarse salt

1 teaspoon ground pepper

1 teaspoon ground cumin

½ teaspoon ground cinnamon

2 beef flank steaks, about 1¼ lb
   (625 g) each

1 bunch fresh cilantro (fresh
   coriander), stems removed

Prepare a hot fire in a grill, or preheat a broiler (griller).

In a cast-iron frying pan over medium-high heat, toast the anchos, turning
often, until fragrant and pliable, 5–7 minutes. Transfer to a cutting board
and discard the stems and seeds. Top the anchos with the garlic, coarse salt,
pepper, cumin, and cinnamon. Chop repeatedly with a large knife until you
have a cohesive mixture. Rub all over the flank steaks.

Place the steaks on the grill rack or under the broiler 4–6 inches (10–
15 cm) from the heat source. Grill or broil, turning once, 4–5 minutes on
each side for medium-rare. Transfer to a cutting board, let stand for 5 minutes, then cut into thin slices against the grain.

Place the cilantro leaves in the center of a large plate and fan the sliced
steaks around the edge. Serve immediately.

serves six | per serving: calories 322 (kilojoules 1,352), protein 37 g, carbohydrates 2 g,
total fat 17 g, saturated fat 7 g, cholesterol 94 mg, sodium 608 mg, dietary fiber 1 g

desserts

blueberry fool

A fool is an old English dessert made of crushed fruit and whipped cream. The traditional favorite is made lighter here with the addition of yogurt. Blackberries or raspberries can be used in place of the blueberries; adjust the amount of sugar as needed.

2 cups (8 oz/250 g) firm but ripe
   blueberries
½ cup (4 oz/125 g) sugar
¼ teaspoon ground cinnamon
1 teaspoon finely grated lemon zest

¼ cup (1¼ oz/37 g) slivered blanched
   almonds
½ cup (4 fl oz/125 ml) heavy
   (double) cream
½ cup (4 oz/125 g) plain yogurt

In a large saucepan, stir together the blueberries, sugar, and cinnamon. Place over high heat, bring to a boil, reduce the heat to medium, and simmer until the berries are soft, 5–7 minutes. Using a fork, crush the berries to a thick, pulpy purée. Remove from the heat and stir in the lemon zest. Transfer to a bowl, cover, and refrigerate until well chilled.

Meanwhile, preheat an oven to 350°F (180°C). Spread the almonds on a baking sheet and toast in the oven until lightly browned and fragrant, about 5 minutes. Remove from the oven and let cool.

In a large bowl, stir together the cream and yogurt. Using an electric mixer set on high speed, beat until thick peaks form. Gently fold in the berry mixture; do not overmix. Spoon into 6 footed glasses such as parfait glasses. Refrigerate for 1–2 hours.

Sprinkle with the toasted almonds just before serving.

serves six | per serving: calories 210 (kilojoules 882), protein 3 g, carbohydrates 27 g, total fat 11 g, saturated fat 5 g, cholesterol 28 mg, sodium 24 mg, dietary fiber 2 g

coffee and bourbon granita

The beauty of a granita for beach house cooking is that you do not need any special equipment—just a metal baking pan or some old ice-cube trays with removable dividers.

3 cups (24 fl oz/750 ml) double-
  strength brewed coffee, preferably
  made from French roast beans

¾ cup (6 oz/185 g) sugar
1½ tablespoons bourbon
whipped cream (optional)

In a large bowl, combine the coffee, sugar, and bourbon and stir to dissolve the sugar. Remove from the heat.

Pour into a metal baking pan large enough to contain the liquid at a depth of 1 inch (2.5 cm) and place in the freezer. When the mixture begins to get icy, after about 1 hour, remove from the freezer and stir well with a fork to break up the ice crystals. Return to the freezer for another 45 minutes. Remove from the freezer and break up the crystals once again. Repeat this process 2 more times until the mixture starts to freeze solid.

To serve, scrape the surface of the granita with the tines of a fork to create ice crystals. Scoop up the crystals and spoon into chilled, small stemmed glasses. Top with a dollop of whipped cream, if desired, and serve at once.

serves six | per serving: calories 123 (kilojoules 517), protein 0 g, carbohydrates 29 g, total fat 0 g, saturated fat 0 g, cholesterol 0 mg, sodium 5 mg, dietary fiber 0 g

figs with sweetened lemon sour cream

Simple yet elegant, this recipe makes an excellent light dessert.
Use unblemished purple or green figs. Serve with slices of Orange and
Almond Cake (page 93) and pour a dessert wine, such as
Sauternes or Beaumes-de-Venise.

½ cup (4 fl oz/125 ml) sour cream
2 tablespoons sugar
1 teaspoon vanilla extract (essence)

1 teaspoon grated lemon zest, plus
long, narrow lemon zest strips
6 large figs

In a small bowl, whisk together the sour cream, sugar, vanilla, and grated lemon zest until smooth. Cover and chill for at least 1 hour or up to 1 day.

Carefully remove the stems from the figs. Stand each fig upright and cut from the top almost to the bottom into quarters. Do not cut all the way through; leave the figs intact at the base. Spread the quarters open like a flower and place on individual plates.

Spoon an equal amount of the sour cream mixture into the center of each fig. Garnish with the lemon zest strips and serve at once.

serves six | per serving: calories 107 (kilojoules 449), protein 1 g, carbohydrates 17 g, total fat 4 g, saturated fat 3 g, cholesterol 8 mg, sodium 11 mg, dietary fiber 2 g

orange and almond cake

¾ cup (3 oz/90 g) sliced (flaked) almonds

2 cups (8 oz/250 g) cake (soft-wheat) flour

1 teaspoon baking powder

¾ cup (6 oz/185 g) unsalted butter, at room temperature

⅓ cup plus 1½ tablespoons (4 oz/125 g) almond paste

1¼ cups (10 oz/310 g) granulated sugar

4 teaspoons finely grated orange zest

1 teaspoon vanilla extract (essence)

6 eggs, at room temperature, separated

1 cup (8 fl oz/250 ml) heavy (double) cream

about ¼ cup (1 oz/30 g) confectioners' (icing) sugar

◯ Preheat an oven to 350°F (180°C). Butter a 9-inch (23-cm) springform pan.

◯ In a food processor, process the almonds until finely chopped. Alternatively, finely chop by hand. Place in a fine-mesh sieve and tap the side to remove the powder. Transfer the almonds to the prepared pan, rotate it to coat the bottom and sides, and tap out any excess.

◯ In a bowl, whisk together the cake flour and baking powder. In a large bowl, using an electric mixer, combine the butter, almond paste, 1 cup (8 oz/250 g) of the granulated sugar, the orange zest, and vanilla. Beat on high speed until light and fluffy, about 10 minutes. Beat in the egg yolks. Divide the flour mixture and the cream into 3 batches each. Add them alternately to the butter mixture, beginning with the flour mixture and folding in each addition until just combined. Do not overmix.

◯ In another large bowl, using clean beaters and with the mixer set on medium speed, beat the egg whites until they mound slightly. Increase the speed to high and gradually beat in the remaining ¼ cup (2 oz/60 g) granulated sugar until soft peaks form. Stir half of the egg whites into the batter to lighten it, then gently fold in the remaining egg whites just until no white streaks remain. Pour into the prepared pan and smooth the top.

◯ Bake until the top is browned and a toothpick inserted into the center comes out clean, about 1 hour. Transfer to a rack and let cool in the pan for 15 minutes. Remove the pan sides and slide the cake onto a rack to cool completely. Transfer to a serving plate and dust the top with confectioners' sugar.

serves six to eight | per serving: calories 797 (kilojoules 3,347), protein 13 g, carbohydrates 81 g, total fat 48 g, saturated fat 23 g, cholesterol 283 mg, sodium 143 mg, dietary fiber 1 g

fresh apricot tart

Use good-quality plain butter cookies if almond cookies are not available. If using a food processor, simply add 2 tablespoons slivered blanched almonds to the crust mixture; if preparing the crust by hand, add ¼ teaspoon almond extract (essence).

½ lb (250 g) butter almond cookies (see note)

3 tablespoons all-purpose (plain) flour

2 tablespoons unsalted butter, cut into pieces

2–3 tablespoons water

⅔ cup (5 oz/155 g) sugar

⅔ cup (5 fl oz/160 ml) heavy (double) cream

3 egg yolks

1 tablespoon amaretto (optional)

12–14 apricots, about 1¾ lb (875 g), halved and pitted

Preheat an oven to 375°F (190°C). In a food processor, combine the cookies and flour and pulse to the consistency of coarse crumbs. Add the butter and pulse briefly to cut it in. Add 2 tablespoons water and pulse again to form a thick dough. If it is not holding together, add the remaining 1 tablespoon water and pulse to blend.

Alternatively, make the crust by hand: In a large lock-top plastic bag, combine the cookies and flour. Force out any excess air and seal. Using a rolling pin, finely crush the cookies. Transfer the cookie crumbs and flour to a large bowl. Using 2 knives or a pastry blender, cut in the butter until the mixture resembles coarse crumbs. Sprinkle with 2 tablespoons of the water, then stir and toss with a fork until a thick dough forms. If the mixture is too dry, add the remaining 1 tablespoon water.

Transfer the mixture to an 8- or 9-inch (20- or 23-cm) quiche or tart pan (do not use one with a removable bottom) and press evenly onto the bottom and up the sides of the pan.

In a bowl, whisk together the sugar, cream, egg yolks, and amaretto, if using, until blended. Arrange the apricot halves, cut sides up, in the lined pan, packing them tightly. Pour the cream mixture evenly over the top.

Bake until the custard is set and the apricots begin to brown, about 45 minutes. Transfer to a rack and let cool completely before slicing.

serves six to eight | per serving: calories 492 (kilojoules 2,066), protein 7 g, carbohydrates 65 g, total fat 23 g, saturated fat 11 g, cholesterol 144 mg, sodium 145 mg, dietary fiber 4 g

orange icebox cookies

Double the recipe and keep wrapped cylinders of dough in the freezer for last-minute treats. Serve with sorbet or ice cream.

½ cup (4 oz/125 g) unsalted butter, at room temperature
½ cup (4 oz/125 g) sugar
1 egg yolk
1½ cups (7½ oz/235 g) all-purpose (plain) flour

1 teaspoon baking powder
⅛ teaspoon salt
¼ cup (2 fl oz/60 ml) orange juice
1 teaspoon finely grated orange zest
8 oz (250 g) good-quality bittersweet chocolate

In a large bowl, using an electric mixer set on high speed, beat together the butter and sugar until light and fluffy. Add the egg yolk and beat until smooth.

In another bowl, sift together the flour, baking powder, and salt and divide into 3 batches. Beat into the butter mixture alternately with the orange juice, beginning and ending with the flour mixture. The dough will be stiff. If it becomes too stiff to beat with a handheld electric mixer, revert to a wooden spoon. Mix in the orange zest.

Place a large sheet of plastic wrap on a work surface. Transfer the dough to the sheet and shape into a long cylinder about 1 inch (2.5 cm) in diameter. Wrap, then twist the ends to seal. Refrigerate for 1 hour.

Preheat an oven to 375°F (190°C). Lightly grease 1 or 2 baking sheets.

Cut the cookies into slices ¼ inch (6 mm) thick and arrange on the baking sheets, spacing them ½ inch (12 mm) apart.

Bake until lightly browned around the edges, about 10 minutes. Transfer to wire racks and let cool completely. Place the chocolate in a heatproof bowl placed over (not touching) simmering water in the lower pan. Melt until smooth, stirring occasionally. Let cool slightly.

Line a baking sheet with waxed paper. Dip one-half of each cookie in the chocolate and place on the lined baking sheet. Refrigerate until the chocolate is firm, about 10 minutes, then gently lift off. Refrigerate between layers of waxed paper in an airtight container for up to 1 week.

makes forty to forty-five small cookies | per cookie: calories 76 (kilojoules 319), protein 1 g, carbohydrates 10 g, total fat 4 g, saturated fat 2 g, cholesterol 11 mg, sodium 19 mg, dietary fiber 0 g

summer pudding

Dark berry juices soak through thin slices of bread to make this
a particularly handsome dessert. If fresh red currants are unavailable,
increase the raspberries by 1 cup (4 oz/125 g) and
reduce the sugar to ⅔ cup (5 oz/155 g).

*8–10 slices fine-textured white
sandwich bread, crusts removed
and cut in half on the diagonal*

3 cups (12 oz/375 g) raspberries

2 cups (8 oz/250 g) blackberries

1 cup (4 oz/125 g) fresh red currants

¾ cup (6 oz/185 g) sugar

2½ teaspoons kirsch or brandy

*1 cup (8 fl oz/250 ml) heavy
(double) cream, whipped*

Line a 1-qt (1-l) pudding mold, soufflé dish, or charlotte mold with the
triangles of bread, arranging them on the bottom so that the pieces fit closely
together. Line the sides with more triangles. Cut out scraps of bread and fit
them into any open spaces. The bowl should be completely lined with bread.

In a large saucepan over medium heat, combine the berries, currants,
and sugar. Bring to a simmer and cook, stirring often, until the berries give
off some of their juice, about 5 minutes. Remove from the heat and stir in
the kirsch or brandy.

Using a slotted spoon, transfer the berries to the lined mold. Pour on
half of the berry juices and reserve the rest. Cover the berries completely
with the remaining bread triangles. Cover any open spaces with scraps of
bread. Trim the bread slices evenly along the top edge.

Place a plate slightly smaller than the diameter of the mold on the bread.
Put the mold in a pan to catch any drips. Set a heavy can or other weight on
the plate and refrigerate for 2 hours. Check the pudding and spoon over a
little of the reserved berry juice if any of the bread slices on top are dry or
white, then refrigerate overnight.

To serve, remove the weight and plate. Run the tip of a small knife
around the sides of the mold and invert the pudding onto a serving plate.
Serve with whipped cream and any reserved berry juices.

serves six | per serving: calories 412 (kilojoules 1,730), protein 5 g, carbohydrates 63 g,
total fat 17 g, saturated fat 9 g, cholesterol 55 mg, sodium 221 mg, dietary fiber 5 g

blackberry cobbler

Strawberries, raspberries, cherries, or blueberries, alone or in combination, can be used in place of the blackberries. Serve the cobbler at room temperature with vanilla ice cream.

for the topping:

1 cup (5 oz/155 g) all-purpose
  (plain) flour

¼ cup (2 oz/60 g) sugar

1 teaspoon baking powder

½ teaspoon salt

¼ cup (2 oz/60 g) chilled unsalted
  butter, cut into small pieces

⅓ cup (3 fl oz/80 ml) milk

for the filling:

6 cups (1½ lb/750 g) blackberries

½ cup (4 oz/125 g) plus 2 tablespoons sugar

2 tablespoons all-purpose (plain)
  flour

1 tablespoon lemon juice

¼ teaspoon ground cinnamon

2 tablespoons unsalted butter, melted

To make the topping, in a large bowl, combine the flour, sugar, baking powder, and salt. Toss with a fork to blend. Using 2 knives or a pastry blender, cut in the butter until the mixture resembles coarse crumbs. Add the milk and, using the fork, stir until a stiff dough forms.

Turn the dough out onto a floured work surface and knead quickly into a ball. It will be sticky. Wrap in plastic wrap and refrigerate for 1 hour.

Flour the work surface and, using a rolling pin or your fingers, spread out the dough into a round ½ inch (12 mm) thick. Using a cookie cutter or wineglass 2½ inches (6 cm) in diameter, cut out 8 rounds.

Preheat an oven to 425°F (220°C). Lightly butter a shallow 2-qt (2-l) baking dish.

To make the filling, in a saucepan over medium-high heat, combine the blackberries, the ½ cup (4 oz/125 g) sugar, flour, lemon juice, and cinnamon. Bring to a boil, remove from the heat, and let cool slightly. Pour into the prepared baking dish, spreading evenly, and arrange the biscuit rounds evenly on top. Brush the rounds with the melted butter and sprinkle the remaining 2 tablespoons sugar over the top.

Bake until the filling is bubbling and the biscuits are golden brown, about 25 minutes. Let cool to room temperature before serving.

serves four to six | per serving: calories 472 (kilojoules 1,982), protein 5 g, carbohydrates 80 g, total fat 16 g, saturated fat 9 g, cholesterol 42 mg, sodium 341 mg, dietary fiber 7 g

melon with lemon sorbet and raspberry sauce

Have all ingredients chilled before assembling. Honeydew melon with lime sorbet makes a nice variation.

2 cups (8 oz/250 g) fresh or thawed
  frozen raspberries

½ cup (2 oz/60 g) confectioners'
  (icing) sugar

1 tablespoon lemon juice

1 cantaloupe, 2–2½ lb (1–1.25 kg),
  halved and seeded

1 pt (16 fl oz/500 ml) premium-
  quality lemon sorbet

fresh mint leaves

In a blender, combine the raspberries, sugar, and lemon juice. Blend for about 30 seconds, scrape down the sides, and blend again until smooth. Transfer to a fine-mesh sieve set over a small bowl. Using the back of a spoon, press the puréed raspberries through the sieve. Cover and chill thoroughly before serving. You should have about 1¼ cups (10 fl oz/310 ml).

Cut each melon half into 4 equal wedges. Using a sharp paring knife, carefully remove and discard the peel. Divide the melon pieces among chilled decorative plates. Top each serving with a scoop of lemon sorbet, and spoon a small amount of the raspberry sauce over the sorbet. Garnish with mint leaves and serve at once. Pass the remaining sauce at the table.

serves four | per serving: calories 239 (kilojoules 1,004), protein 2 g, carbohydrates 60 g, total fat 1 g, saturated fat 0 g, cholesterol 0 mg, sodium 24 mg, dietary fiber 4 g

sour cherry crisp

Tart, intensely flavorful sour cherries are at their peak for only a short time in the summer. Canned or bottled cherries (packed in water) can be used out of season. Serve with plenty of vanilla ice cream.

7 oz (220 g) frozen puff pastry,
thawed

1 egg lightly beaten with 1 teaspoon
warm water

4 cups (10 oz/315 g) pitted sour
cherries

¾ cup (6 oz/185 g) sugar

¼ cup (1½ oz/45 g) all-purpose
(plain) flour

1 tablespoon lemon juice

2 tablespoons unsalted butter,
cut into pieces

On a floured work surface, roll out the pastry dough into an 8-by-12-inch (20-by-30-cm) rectangle about ⅛ inch (3 mm) thick. Place a 1½-qt (1.5-l) baking dish upside down on the dough. Using a sharp knife, carefully trace the outer edge of the dish; the dough must have exactly the same dimensions as the top of the dish. Set the dish aside.

Transfer the dough to a baking sheet and brush the pastry lightly with some of the egg-water mixture. Prick all over with a fork, cover with plastic wrap, and refrigerate for 30 minutes.

Preheat an oven to 375°F (190°C).

In a saucepan, combine the cherries, sugar, flour, and lemon juice. Stir well. Place over medium-high heat and cook until thickened, stirring occasionally, about 10 minutes. Remove from the heat, stir in the butter, and pour into the reserved baking dish. Set aside.

Remove the baking sheet from the refrigerator and brush the pastry with the remaining egg-water mixture. Bake until lightly golden and puffed, about 12 minutes. Using a wide spatula, carefully transfer the pastry to the baking dish, covering the cherry filling fully. Press down lightly.

Bake until the filling is bubbling and the pastry is crisp and golden brown, about 30 minutes. Transfer to a rack and let cool slightly before serving.

serves six to eight | per serving: calories 337 (kilojoules 1,415), protein 4 g, carbohydrates 48 g, total fat 15 g, saturated fat 4 g, cholesterol 39 mg, sodium 82 mg, dietary fiber 0 g

panna cotta with strawberries and plums

Panna cotta ("cooked cream" in Italian) is like a baked custard without the eggs. Here, plums and strawberries dress up the dessert. You can substitute currants for the strawberries and green plums for the red ones.

2 cups (16 fl oz/500 ml) heavy (double) cream

1 cup (8 fl oz/250 ml) milk

½ cup (2 oz/60 g) confectioners' (icing) sugar

5 lemon zest strips, each 3 inches (7.5 cm) long

1 vanilla bean, split in half lengthwise, or ¾ teaspoon vanilla extract (essence)

3¾ teaspoons unflavored gelatin

8 plums, about 1½ lb (750 g) total weight, pitted and thinly sliced

1 pt (8 oz/250 g) strawberries, halved

In a saucepan over medium-high heat, combine the cream, ⅔ cup (5 fl oz/160 ml) of the milk, the confectioners' sugar, the lemon zest, and the vanilla bean, if using. Bring to a simmer, stirring often. Remove from the heat, cover, and set aside for 10 minutes. Meanwhile, in a small bowl, combine the remaining ⅓ cup (3 fl oz/90 ml) milk and the gelatin. Set aside to soften for about 10 minutes.

Bring the cream mixture back to a simmer. Remove from the heat and whisk in the gelatin mixture until smooth. Strain through a fine-mesh sieve set over a large measuring pitcher. Stir in the vanilla extract, if using.

Pour into six ¾-cup (6–fl oz/180-ml) custard cups or ramekins. Cover and chill until set, about 3 hours.

To serve, run a small knife around the edge of each cup and unmold onto individual serving plates. Arrange the plum slices and strawberry halves around the molds. Serve at once.

serves six | per serving: calories 422 (kilojoules 1,772), protein 6 g, carbohydrates 33 g, total fat 31 g, saturated fat 19 g, cholesterol 114 g, sodium 53 mg, dietary fiber 2 g

peaches poached in sauternes

4 firm but ripe peaches
ice water to cover
1 teaspoon lemon juice
½ cup (4 oz/120 g) sugar
1½ cups (12 fl oz/375 ml) Sauternes
  or similar sweet wine

1 lemon zest strip, about 2 inches
  (5 cm) long
½ vanilla bean, split lengthwise
fresh mint leaves

Bring a saucepan three-fourths full of water to a boil. Plunge the peaches into the boiling water for about 30 seconds, then transfer to a bowl of ice water, let cool, and slip off the skins. Halve the peaches, discard the pits, and place the halves in a bowl. Sprinkle with the lemon juice and ¼ cup (2 oz/60 g) of the sugar. Stir to coat. Set aside for 30 minutes.

In a large saucepan over high heat, combine the remaining ¼ cup (2 oz/ 60 g) sugar, the wine, lemon zest, and vanilla bean. Bring to a boil, stirring just until the sugar dissolves. Reduce the heat to medium. Add the peach halves and cook, uncovered, until tender, 5–10 minutes. Using a slotted spoon, transfer the peaches to a glass dish; reserve the liquid in the pan. Let the peaches cool completely. Bring the poaching liquid to a boil and cook rapidly until reduced to ¾ cup (6 fl oz/180 ml). Strain through a fine-mesh sieve into a separate bowl and let cool. Cover the peaches and liquid and chill well, at least 2 hours or up to 1 day.

Divide the peaches among chilled dessert glasses and garnish with mint leaves. Spoon an equal amount of the poaching syrup over each serving.

serves four | per serving: calories 170 (kilojoules 714), protein 1 g, carbohydrates 44 g, total fat 0 g, saturated fat 0 g, cholesterol 0 mg, sodium 5 mg, dietary fiber 2 g

index

acknowledgments

The publishers and photography team wish to thank, in San Francisco, Beverly and Andy Stern, Sue Fisher King, Sandra Griswold, Pottery Barn, and Williams-Sonoma; in Stinson Beach, Seadrift Co; in Bermuda, Judy Montgomery-Moore, Mr. and Mrs. deForest Trimingham, John and Nancy Wadson, Hubert and Penny Watlington, The Coral Beach & Tennis Club, Tom and Nancy Wadson, Chef Stephan Juliusburger, Doug Gibbs, and Anthony Mello.

additional photography

Pages 4-5 © Walter Bibikow/FPG International, pages 8-9 © Gene Ahrens/FPG International.